# WHAT HAPPENS WHEN YOU DIE?

# What Happens When You Die?

## A Biblical Perspective

Clement C. Butler

RESOURCE *Publications* · Eugene, Oregon

WHAT HAPPENS WHEN YOU DIE?
A Biblical Perspective

Copyright © 2021 Clement C. Butler. All rights reserved. Except for brief quotations in critical publications or reviews, no part of this book may be reproduced in any manner without prior written permission from the publisher. Write: Permissions, Wipf and Stock Publishers, 199 W. 8th Ave., Suite 3, Eugene, OR 97401.

Resource Publications
An Imprint of Wipf and Stock Publishers
199 W. 8th Ave., Suite 3
Eugene, OR 97401

www.wipfandstock.com
PAPERBACK ISBN:
978-1-6667-1754-9 HARDCOVER
ISBN: 978-1-6667-1755-6 EBOOK
ISBN: 978-1-6667-1756-3
Unless otherwise indicated, Scripture references are taken from the King James Version of

the Bible. Please send comments and questions to approvedworkmanministries@yahoo.com

Please visit our website: www.approvedworkmanministries.com

Follow us on Twitter @242teacher

# Contents

Acknowledgments .................................................................. vii
Preface .................................................................................... ix
Introduction ........................................................................... xi

Chapter 1   A Living Soul ...................................................... 1
   Man was Made from the Dust of the Earth ................... 2
   God Breathed the Breath of Life into Man .................... 6
   Definitions of Breath ........................................................ 9
   Man Became a Living Soul ............................................. 11
   Soul and Spirit: The Difference ...................................... 13
   The Immortality of the Soul? ......................................... 15
   We Are Spirit Beings ....................................................... 19

Chapter 2   Those Who Have Fallen Asleep ...................... 21
   Resurrection: Awakening From Sleep ........................... 24
   Enoch ................................................................................ 25
   Elijah ................................................................................. 26
   Moses ................................................................................ 28
   Has Anyone Gone to Heaven? ........................................ 31

Chapter 3   The First and Second Resurrections .............. 33
   The First Resurrection .................................................... 34
   Firstfruits of them Which Slept ..................................... 41
   The Resurrected Body ..................................................... 43
   A Blink, A Wink, And A Twinkle ................................. 47
   In This Tent, We Groan .................................................. 48

    The Second Resurrection ..................................................50
    Christ's Resurrection and His Body......................................55

Chapter 4   I Go To Prepare A Place For You ............................60
    What is the Context and Perspective of the Passage?.................62
    What Is the Father's House? ..................................................66
    Based on the Context of the Passage, What are Mansions? .......68
    I Go to Prepare a Place for You .............................................70
    I Will Come Again and Receive You unto Myself...................71
    Where Will Believers Spend Eternity?....................................73

Chapter 5   Heaven and Hell..................................................79
    Heaven ................................................................................80
    The First Heaven .................................................................82
    The Second Heaven .............................................................84
    The Third Heaven................................................................85
    Hell .....................................................................................87
    Hades ..................................................................................88
    Tartaroo ..............................................................................89
    Gehenna..............................................................................90

Chapter 6   Abraham's Bosom ................................................92
    Abraham's Bosom................................................................97
    Today You Shall Be With Me In Paradise ............................100
    Heaven .............................................................................. 101
    Hell (The side of torments- where the rich man went)............ 102
    Paradise ............................................................................ 105
    The Spirits in Prison ......................................................... 105
    Absent From The Body, Present With The Lord...................107
    The Spirits of Just Men Made Perfect................................. 109
    God's Promise to Abraham................................................ 112
    Paradise and Its Present Location....................................... 113

Conclusion.................................................................................... 115
References ..................................................................................... 116
About the Author........................................................................... 119

**CONTENDERS FOR THE FAITH**

# Acknowledgments

This book is dedicated to every believer looking forward to the blessed hope and the glorious appearance of the great God and our Savior Jesus Christ. Everyone who has this hope in them would purify themselves even as He is pure.

Special thanks to Glenroy Pratt, Pastor Arthur Evans, Dorethea Moss, Diana Bowe, and Heath Fowler.

# Preface

In Benjamin Franklin's letter to Jean Baptiste-Leroy in 1789, he said, "In this world, nothing can be said to be certain, except death and taxes." This sentiment was also echoed in the movie, "Meet Joe Black," where the character Drew says to Joe Black, "We all know this deal is as certain as death and taxes." Joe's response was, "What an odd pairing!" Indeed, it is an odd pairing. However, of the two, I submit that death is more definite because certain taxes can be modified or, in some cases, eliminated.

As a whole, many things in life are uncertain. We make plans, set agendas, and establish goals. While these are all good and healthy for our progression, they are all also subject to our mortal existence. From the moment we are born, the clock begins to tick, and we are all on an inevitable path to death. In fact, it is an appointment or a reservation to which we are all destined. Hebrews 9:27 says, "It is appointed unto men once to die, but after this the judgment." Furthermore, in relation to death, Ecclesiastes 9:2-3 says this is the one event that happens to us all. Therefore, it is an appointment to which we all have been foreordained.

According to Ecology Global Network, on average, 55.3 million people die each year around the world. This figure is further broken down into smaller units with 151,600 dying each day; 6,316 people dying each hour; 105 people dying each minute and nearly two people dying each second. Furthermore, the average life expectancy is approximately 67 years. Therefore, the assurance of death is definite.

Not only is death a certainty, but the Bible also points to the brevity or succinctness of life. James compares it to a vapor or smoke that appears for a little while and then vanishes away (James 4:13-15). Also, 1 Peter 1:24 establishes an analogy equating our lives to the grass of the field and the glory of man to the flower of the grass. The grass fades or loses its luster and the flower falls away, foregoing the hallmark of its beauty.

Another reference, Psalm 103:16 adds that when this occurs, the place where the grass was planted no longer remembers it. From a contemporary point of view, the group Kansas in their song entitled "Dust in the Wind," says that as human beings, "All we are is dust in the wind." Though I don't subscribe to the song's implication of the futility of life, it certainly is aligned with the concept of the shortness of our lives like that of vapor.

I ask you, except for a few individuals who history will record, will anyone remember who you were a hundred years from now? Death certainly has a way of erasing even the memory of us. We work feverishly in life establishing a name for ourselves and exert great effort to accomplish the things we deem important. Yet, with all the glory of our achievements, they all fade and wither in death. Therefore, let us labor, not for that which perishes and fades away, but for that which endures to everlasting life.

Clement C. Butler
Author

# Introduction

From the 1938 movie, "Dead Men Tell No Tales," an English schoolteacher wins a French lottery. However, on her way to Paris to collect the money, she is murdered, and an imposter claims her prize. Based on the movie, the notion is that once you are dead, you can no longer communicate, reveal secrets, or tell tales. Further to this, is the understanding that the dead cannot convey what it is like to be dead. Moreover, Ecclesiastes 9:5 says, "For the living know that they shall die: but the dead know not anything." If the dead know nothing and cannot communicate with the living, then by what account is it determined what happens after death?

Is this life all there is, or can we expect something else once we cross the threshold of death? Do we subscribe to the notion of YOLO (You Only Live Once)? This is certainly not a new question or discussion as the responses or practices surrounding death have persisted from the dawn of time. In fact, they have plagued mankind for as long as the earth has stood, and even after several millenniums, a clear answer still seems to be evasive. Furthermore, various religions and cultures have even implemented elaborate systems based on their persuasions concerning the afterlife. A great example is the ancient Egyptians who had an intricate system to prepare them for life after death. The process included mummification to preserve the physical body in addition to being buried with valuables and necessities deemed essential for the next life. From these practices to the concept of reincarnation, the fascination with life after death has and will continue to be a topical discussion.

In that vein, what does the Word of God have to say concerning what happens when we die or life after death? Let me be clear! This book is not based on someone's dream, vision, near-death experience, or a cunningly devised fable. As with most infallible offerings, there must be parameters or boundaries that make the distinction between what is factual and what is unfounded. While the subject of death and what happens thereafter may have a mysterious undertone, the "more sure" word of prophecy or the Word of God is quite clear about what happens when we die. Unfortunately, reality has been bartered for fantasy and truth has been compromised in the name of emotional comfort.

This book intends to provide clarity concerning this all-important subject from a biblical perspective and hopefully eliminate perceptions regarding death that cannot be supported by Scripture. To accomplish this, the text begins by explaining how we are configured as human beings along with highlighting the difference between body, soul, and spirit. It also offers a detailed account of what happens to each of these parts when we die. This is followed by why the Bible uses sleep to describe death along with a discussion on the first and second death and the first and second resurrection. Also, included in this exchange is clarification on where believers will spend eternity. While on this subject, the topic of mansions in heaven is also taken into account. Finally, the book addresses the distinctions between heaven and hell, discusses Abraham's Bosom and explains where Jesus went when He died. Upon reading this book, you will find that it offers one of the more comprehensive perspectives of the subject of death, addressing a myriad of topics related to what happens when we die.

One of my favorite movies of all time is "Gladiator." In the movie, the Roman general, Maximus Decimus Meridus, portrayed by Russell Crowe says, "What we do in life echoes in eternity." How true and profound this statement is as the reverberations of our actions will still be heard even after we utter our last words. As transparency often brings with it comfort, I firmly believe that a better understanding of death and what transpires afterward will aid in the type of life we live and the decisions we make. In completing this volume, I had to abandon many long-held persuasions based on the enlightenment from Scripture. I have found that truth, which can stand the test of scriptural scrutiny and prevail, is better appreciated than doctrine simply accepted based on traditions and emotions. It is my prayer that as you read and study this work, you would allow the same transformation to occur, so that which cannot be shaken will inevitably remain.

## Chapter One

# A Living Soul

Tremendous value can be found in examining the beginning of something to gain a better understanding concerning the end of it. For this reason, we will follow this pattern and establish a proper foundation, for it is agreed that life precedes death.

In providing a scriptural perspective of what happens after death, it is fundamental to begin with the essence of life. Accordingly, to determine what happens with human beings after death, our composition must first be established. This is revealed in the book of Genesis regarding our creation. The point is if we do not understand how we were configured from our creation, we would be at a disadvantage to explain what happens when we die. The account of our creation is recorded in Genesis 2:7:

> And the LORD God formed man of the dust of the ground, and breathed into his nostrils the breath of life, and man became a living soul.

Let us examine precisely the three things that this passage is conveying.

1. Man (mankind in a general sense or humanity) was made (fashioned or framed) from the dust of the ground (earth).

2. The breath of God was breathed into man (his nostrils) and this was the breath necessary for life.

3. Man became a living soul. As it relates to the word "soul," Genesis 2:7 says specifically that man **became** a living soul).

Without a clear grasp of these three constituents of man and how they relate to our existence, the discussion of death and life after death will never draw dependable conclusions. Therefore, let us look at these three aspects in greater detail.

## 1. MAN WAS MADE FROM THE DUST OF THE EARTH

The word "dust" is the Hebrew word *aphar*, which means:

- Dry earth
- Powder
- Ashes
- Earth
- Ground
- Mortar

The word "ground" is the Hebrew word *adamah*, which means:

- Earth substance (for building or constructing)
- Ground as earth's visible surface
- Land, territory, country

Notice that within the Hebrew word for ground (*adamah*) is the word "Adam." This indicates that the very substance that Adam (humanity in general) was made from was dry earth or the dust of the ground. Adam was a terrestrial being. Therefore, his substance or the material he was made from was of the earth. He was an earthy being—designed for the earth and made from the earth.

Let us look at several passages of Scripture, which reiterate that our body is natural and was made from the dust of the earth.

> In the sweat of thy face shalt thou eat bread, till thou return unto the ground; for out of it wast thou taken: for dust thou art, and unto dust shalt thou return. (Genesis 3:19)

> And Abraham answered and said, Behold now, I have taken upon me to speak unto the Lord, which am but dust and ashes. (Genesis 18:27)

> Remember, I beseech thee, that thou hast made me as the clay; and wilt thou bring me into dust again? (Job 10:9)

> For he knoweth our frame; he remembereth that we are dust. (Psalm 103:14)

> All go unto one place; all are of the dust, and all turn to dust again. (Ecclesiastes 3:20)

> Then shall the dust return to the earth as it was: and the spirit shall return unto God who gave it. (Ecclesiastes 12:7)

In using the name Adam as a representative figure, 1 Corinthians 15:45-49 makes a distinction between the first Adam and the last Adam. The first Adam is the one from the garden of Eden and the last Adam is Jesus Christ. Therefore, in a figurative sense, Scripture identifies two Adams with each one representing something different.

> 45. And so it is written, the first man Adam was <u>made a living soul</u>; the last Adam was <u>made a quickening spirit.</u>

46. Howbeit that was not first which is spiritual, but that which is natural; and afterward that which is spiritual.

47. The first man is of the earth, earthy: the second man is the Lord from heaven.

48. As is the earthy, such are they also that are earthy: and as is the heavenly, such are they also that are heavenly.

49. And as we have borne the image of the earthy, we shall also bear the image of the heavenly. (1 Corinthians 15:45-49)

The comparison offered in the above passage is relative to the substance or essence of each Adam, as well as the composition of their material bodies, which is the context of the chapter. A parallel of the contrast is outlined in the table below.

Table 1

| FIRST ADAM | LAST ADAM |
|---|---|
| Living Soul<br>Again, as it relates to the word "soul," it says specifically that he was made a living soul. That is who he was. | Quickening Spirit<br>It does not say that Jesus has a quickening spirit but that He *is* a quickening (life-giving) Spirit. That is who He is. |
| Natural | Spiritual |
| Of the earth, earthy | The Lord from heaven, heavenly |
| Earthy and produces after its kind (earthy). According to the law of reproduction, each seed produces after its kind (Genesis 1:11). | Heavenly and produces after His kind. As is the heavenly, such are they who are heavenly. |

| We have borne the image of the earthy, in terms of our bodies. It is natural and of the earth (earthy). This body based on the law of reproduction was produced after the kind that Adam had (of the dust of the ground). | We shall also bear the image of the heavenly. However, this body is neither of the earth nor is it earthy. This body based on the law of reproduction is heavenly. It is similar to Jesus' resurrected body. |
|---|---|

In light of the entire context of 1 Corinthians Chapter 15, which is the resurrection of the body, the complete chapter is designed to emphasize the kind of body believers will have in the resurrection. It does this by making the distinction between a natural/earthy body and a spiritual/heavenly body.

The first Adam was made from the dust of the ground. Therefore, he had a natural/earthy body, which is what every human presently has. The first Adam produced after his kind and could only give or reproduce from the substance he possessed. On the other hand, the last Adam, after His resurrection, had a spiritual body. This resembles the type of body believers will have in the first resurrection. Hence, as we have borne the earthy image, we shall also bear the heavenly image.

The principle of the Word of God is that the natural always precedes the spiritual, which is also true concerning the discussion of bodies (1 Corinthians 15:46). First, there is a natural body and afterward, there will be a spiritual body. The distinction is therefore clear: the first Adam being made from the dust of the earth is earthy and, at present, in terms of our physical bodies, we bear his earthy image. In accordance with the law of reproduction, Adam produced after his kind; therefore, all humans have bodies made from the dust of the earth.

## 2. God Breathed the Breath of Life into Man

Initially, when the Lord formed Adam from the dust of the ground, he was just lying there; he had no life. Genesis 2:7 says that after his body was completely framed, God breathed the breath of life into his nostrils. What exactly is the breath of life? Based on the foundational principles that were laid in my book *The Volume of the Book: Insights into Rightly Dividing the Word of Truth*, it was underscored that Scripture interprets Scripture or simply put, the Bible interprets itself. Furthermore, as principles go, Genesis 2:7 serves as a reference to "the first mention principle." The principle states that to establish a particular doctrine or understand a certain subject from the Bible, you have to go to the place in Scripture where the topic was first mentioned. This often serves as a foundation for its usage throughout the Bible although there are some exceptions. Based on this principle, the Bible introduces the subject in its basic form and then elaborates on it throughout Scripture. A particular doctrine can then be followed from the beginning to the end with increasing knowledge. This is referred to as the progressive mention principle.

The "first mention principle" is most obvious when the term "as it is written" is used in the Bible. As Genesis 2:7 contains the first time the term "breath of life" is mentioned in Scripture, this represents our starting point. Therefore, all the other scriptures that speak to the breath of life springboard from this one. Moreover, as the Bible is a progressive book, the subsequent references often provide more clarity and a better understanding of what is being said, whereas the first mentioned Scripture may not have provided elaborate details.

Additionally, to establish precisely what is being said in the Bible, all the passages related to the particular subject have to be examined. As a principle, this is referred to as "the whole of Scripture context." This is why studying requires discipline and takes time. Let us look at several passages of Scripture that not only support Genesis 2:7 but also provide a better understanding of the term "breath of life."

> And, behold, I, even I, do bring a flood of waters upon the earth, to destroy all flesh, wherein is the breath of life, from under heaven; and everything that is in the earth shall die. (Genesis 6:17)

> And it came to pass after these things, that the son of the woman, the mistress of the house, fell sick; and his sickness was so sore, that there was no breath left in him. (1 Kings 17:17)

> In whose hand (God) is the soul of every living thing, and the breath of all mankind. (Job 12:10)

> All the while my breath is in me, and the spirit (breath) of God is in my nostrils. (Job 27:3)

> The Spirit of God hath made me, and the breath of the Almighty hath given me life. (Job 33:4)

5. Thus saith the Lord GOD unto these bones; Behold, I will cause breath to enter into you, and ye shall live:

6. And I will lay sinews upon you, and will bring up flesh upon you, and cover you with skin, and put breath in you, and ye shall live; and ye shall know that I am the LORD. (Ezekiel 37:5, 6)

When we take into account what the above scriptures are saying, in conjunction with what is mentioned in Genesis 2:7, we have a better perspective regarding the breath of life. In combination, they convey that the breath, which is essential for the life of all humanity came from God. His breath causes us to live. It is His breath that made us alive and when this breath leaves our bodies, we die. As breath is vital for life, let us examine the word "breath" in detail.

From Genesis 2:7, the word "breathed" is the Hebrew word *naphach,* which means to blow. Therefore, God blew into man "the breath of life." He did not command it; He blew it into Adam's nostrils. All during creation, the Lord spoke the material world into existence. During the first chapter of Genesis, we repeatedly see the phrase, "And God said" followed by, "And it was so." However, when it came to humanity, God said in Genesis 1:26, "Let us make man," which denotes a personal touch as opposed to simply speaking things into being. As mentioned in Genesis 2:7, even after the man was made or framed, God "blew" into him the breath of life. Thus, this demonstrated a more personal touch and the consideration which the Creator has for humanity. Hence, the creation of man was an intimate undertaking. He is, indeed, mindful of us (Job 7:17, Psalm 8:4-8). In addition, God breathing into man typified the principle that *the breath of God produces life or without His breath, there is no life.* In reference to the first Adam, this produced natural life. However, concerning salvation, the breath of God or the Holy Spirit produces spiritual life. When God breathed into Adam, He created a living soul or a living creature. Based on this principle, when God breathes His Holy Spirit into those who accept Him, He creates a new creature or a new person (2 Corinthians 5:17).

To support the principle that we receive spirit or life by the breath of God, John 20:21-22 says,

> 21. Then said Jesus to them again, Peace be unto you: as my Father hath sent me, even so send I you.
>
> 22. And when he had said this, <u>he breathed on them, and saith unto them, Receive ye the Holy Ghost.</u>

When God breathed into Adam, he received spirit and was made alive. Similarly, when God breathes His Spirit into those that accept Him, they are also made alive. Therefore, the point is that, in both instances, *the breath of God produces life.* To be clear, the spirit or breath that the first Adam received was not the Holy Spirit. What God breathed into him was simply the breath of life or the breath necessary for him to be alive (Genesis 2:7). To reiterate the point, the principle is that breath from God provides the essence of life. In the example of Adam, it was natural life. However, for those who receive the Holy Spirit, this produces spiritual life.

As it pertains to the first Adam, let us look at what constitutes the term "breath of life." In the Old Testament, there are two Hebrew words for the word "breath," which are *neshamah* and *ruwach*.

## DEFINITIONS OF BREATH

*Neshamah* means the following:

- Wind (Genesis 2:7)
- Blast (Genesis 4:9, Psalm 18:15)
- Spirit (Job 26:4, Job 27:3, Proverbs 20:27)
- Inspiration (Job 32:8)
- Soul (life) (Isaiah 57:16)

In particular, let us look at Job 26:4 and Job 27:3 as they offer greater specificity to this discussion.

> To whom hast thou uttered words? and whose spirit came from thee? (Job 26:4)

> All the while my breath is in me, and the spirit of God is in my nostrils. (Job 27:3)

*Ruwach* means the following:

- Spirit (of God) (Genesis 1:2, Genesis 6:3, Isaiah 44:3, Isaiah 61:1)
- Cool (wind) (Genesis 3:8)
- Spirit (of man/life) (Genesis 41:8, Genesis 45:27, Joshua 2:11) (that which causes animation, vitality, vigor, courage). Spirit of the living. That which leaves man at death
- Wind (Genesis 8:1, Exodus 10:13, Psalm 1:4, Psalm 78:39)
- Mind (seat of emotion or mental acts) (Genesis 26:35, Numbers 5:30, Judges 8:3)
- Blast (Exodus 15:8)
- Air (Job 41:16)
- Tempest/Whirlwind (Psalm 11:6, Ezekiel 1:4)

Based on the definitions of the word "breath," when God breathed "the breath of life" into Adam, he received air or wind that enabled him to have a natural life, to become animated, or come alive. Note that the origin of life is from God and without this breath from Him, Adam was simply an earthy shell. This is why, in reference to death and the breath of life, Ecclesiastes 12:7 says, "Then shall the dust return to the Earth as it was: and the spirit shall return unto God who gave it."

The breath of God produced the essence of our lives, which is referred to as spirit. Of note, the breath we receive is not just oxygen; it is life itself. This is also evident through our exhalation of this breath. When we exhale, we demonstrate that we are happy, sad, tired, miserable, etc. Additionally, you find that the two words (breath and spirit) are often used interchangeably throughout Scripture. Therefore, based on Ecclesiastes 12:7, when we die, our bodies go back to the earth (our material substance) and our spirits (our immaterial substance), which came from God, simply go back to Him. Hence, everything goes back to where it originated.

Furthermore, James 2:26 supports this premise and says: "For as the body without the spirit is dead, so faith without works is dead." The word "spirit" is the Greek word *pneuma*, which means breath (breath of life). Therefore, once the spirit or breath of God leaves the body, the body dies. This is the same breath of life that is essential for natural life, which Genesis 2:7 speaks of.

With the term breath of life in Genesis 2:7 representing the first mention principle, the word "spirit" in both Ecclesiastes 12:7 and James 2:26 adds more insight to the subject. Therefore, God gave man the breath of life or spirit, which provided life. This was exhibited by the fact that man became animated and had the capacity to perform emotional and mental acts. By definition, this is what Genesis 2:7 refers to as a living soul. The breath of life gave man natural life and the ability to become a living soul. As it pertains to the configuration of man, this brings us to the third point that is derived from Genesis 2:7.

## 3. Man Became a Living Soul

To have a better understanding of what happens at death, we must appreciate the relationship between the body, soul, and spirit. Furthermore, as stated at the beginning of this chapter, to grasp what happens at death, the genesis or beginning of life has to be understood.

So far in our discussion, we have covered in detail the body, which was made from the earth, along with the spirit, which was given by the breath of God. This next conversation will shed light on the living soul, which Scripture identifies as the combination of body and spirit. See Exhibit 1.

Exhibit 1

Genesis 2:7 says that after the Lord formed Adam from the dust of the ground (body), He breathed into him the breath of life (spirit), and he became a living soul. Notice that this particular scripture, which lays the foundation for this discussion on the soul doesn't say that man was given a soul but rather that he **"became"** a living (lively or alive) soul. The word "became" means that he came into **being** (as opposed to having). It stands to reason, therefore, that "soul" is not something we possess; rather, it is who we are as human beings. We are living souls.

What does Genesis 2:7 mean when it says that man became a living soul? In simple language, it means he became alive; he was given life. He became animated and was now an expressive being who was able to display emotions and have mental capacity.

A soul, therefore, is a living being. It is an identifiable person or individual. Based on what we have covered in this chapter, it is a combination of an earthy body and the breath of life (spirit). In other words, the breath of life from God entering the earthy body created a living soul called man. Hence, when breathing ceases, the living soul we are also ceases to exist. For example, if I refer to the late Nelson Mandela, I'm not referring to his spirit or his true existence but his identification as a living soul or an identifiable person.

In Genesis 2:7, the word "soul" is the Hebrew word *nephesh* and means the following:

- A living being (Genesis 12:5, 13)
- A breathing/living creature (Genesis 9:12)
- The man himself, self, person or individual (Genesis 17:14, Genesis 27:4, Leviticus 22:11, Leviticus 23:30, 1 Kings 17:22, Psalm 23:3, Proverbs 6:32, Isaiah 53:10,11, Matthew 10:28, Matthew 16:26, Luke 12:19-20, Acts 2:43)
- Seat of appetites, emotions, and passion (Genesis 34:3, Genesis 42:21, Leviticus 26:15, Deuteronomy 13:3, Judges 16:16, 1 Samuel 1:10, 1 Samuel 18:1, Psalm 42:2)

- The activity of the mind (1 Samuel 2:35, 1 Chronicles 28:9, Jeremiah 15:1, Ezekiel 23:28)
- Heart (Exodus 23:9, Deuteronomy 24:15)
- Life (Genesis 19:17-19, Genesis 32:30, Genesis 35:18, Exodus 12:15)

In referring to Noah and his family surviving the flood, 1 Peter 3:20 says that eight souls (lives) were saved. Therefore, based on the definition that Scripture provides, we can conclude that a living soul as it relates to man is simply a living being or a person. This individual has the capacity to exhibit desires, thoughts, and passions, which are activities of the heart and mind. A living soul is a living being able to think and have an intellect. It is mortal life itself, a state of consciousness and all that that entails.

When we exhibit our desires or thoughts, the substance of our inner lives or spirits is observable. Soul, therefore, is the vehicle through which the spirit on the inside expresses itself on the outside. The person you are on the inside is expressed or observed through exhalation; this is seen as a soulish display.

Throughout Scripture, the words "soul" and "spirit" are often used interchangeably. However, based on the above explanation, there is indeed, a difference.

## SOUL AND SPIRIT: THE DIFFERENCE

It is a commonly accepted concept that we are spirits; we have souls and live in bodies. However, based on our study to this point, we can conclude that this is not an entirely accurate perspective of our composition as human beings. As it pertains to our whole person, we are, indeed, body, soul, and spirit as stated in 1 Thessalonians 5:23. The body, as we have determined, is the physical self, made from the earth. Our spirit is the essence of life given to us by the breath of God. Spirit was breathed into man and represents the life of the person. It is who we are on the inside.

A living soul, therefore, is the combination of body and spirit. It is who we are as individuals. It is how we are identified by the world or those around us. It proclaims the person or the substance we are on the inside. Your soul expresses the personality and character of your spirit or inner life. This describes the distinction between the two. Thus, a reclassification of our configuration is that we are spirits who live in bodies. The expression or exhibition of this is referred to as a living soul.

When we become born again by the Holy Spirit, our spirits or very lives are regenerated. Moreover, it is with our spirits that we commune with God. This is how we contact and receive from God. Furthermore, it is by our spirits that we are joined to the Lord, and we become one spirit with Him (1 Corinthians 6:17). Hence, those who are not born again by God's Spirit, though they have natural life (spirit), are still spiritually dead because they are not connected to the Father or one with Him. This is why Ephesians 2:1 describes being born again as being quickened (made alive).

It has been explained in detail what it means to be a living soul. Additionally, we have also expanded on what the spirit is. As mentioned earlier, sometimes in Scripture, we notice that the word "soul" is used as a synonym for "spirit." They are used interchangeably. For example, 1 John 4:1 in referring to false prophets admonishes us not to believe every spirit, meaning the actual person. However, the exercise that we have just undertaken clearly highlights the distinction between soul and spirit. On that note, Hebrews Chapter 4 points out that distinguishing between the two is complicated and can only be differentiated by using the Word of God.

> For the word of God is quick, and powerful, and sharper than any two-edged sword, piercing even *to the dividing asunder of soul and spirit,* and of the joints and marrow, and is a discerner of the thoughts and intents of the heart (Hebrews 4:12).

Just as there is a difference between the thoughts of the heart compared to its intent, even though they both involve a similar process, there is also a distinction between the soul and the spirit though they are also intertwined. The essence of the life you possess, the person on the inside (spirit) will be exhibited by means of the soul.

## THE IMMORTALITY OF THE SOUL?

The word "immortality" suggests that something is everlasting or not subject to death. However, in many references where the Bible refers to man as a soul or uses the word "soul" in a general sense, there is no indication of its immortality. Unless, in the instances where the word "soul" is being used as an alternative to the word "spirit" (Matthew 10:28, Revelation 20:4), soul primarily refers to a living, mortal person.

If the breath of life (spirit) entering the body produced a living soul (Genesis 2:7), then the exiting of the breath of life from the body (James 2:26) causes the living soul or the individual to die. Again, I reiterate that the soul is not a separate being from the body but simply a combination of body and spirit. It is used as the expression of our inner lives. This combination produces a natural, mortal product, which is a living mortal soul called man. Therefore, apart from its occasional substitution with spirit, the specific terminology of an immortal soul is not supported by Scripture. In fact, the predominant communication of the Bible is that our spirits are immortal and immaterial. This is the life produced by the breath of God, and it is eternal in nature. Thus, death is the separation of our spirits from our natural bodies. It is the separation of the immaterial from the material. Hence, what dies is the material part of us or our earthy bodies. 2 Corinthians 5:1 characterizes death as the dissolving or the taking off of our earthy houses. The body, therefore, serves as the housing or tabernacle for our spirits.

1. For we know that if our earthly house of this tabernacle were dissolved, we have a building of God, an house not made with hands, eternal in the heavens.

2. For in this we groan, earnestly desiring to be clothed upon with our house which is from heaven:

3. If so be that being clothed we shall not be found naked.

4. For we that are in this tabernacle do groan, being burdened: not for that we would be unclothed, but clothed upon, that mortality might be swallowed up of life. (2 Corinthians 5:1-4)

According to Scripture, when our bodies die, our spirits are in a state of being "unclothed' or "naked." We put off our housing. In light of this, as it pertains to our bodies or houses, the passage creates a comparison between two distinct houses. It compares that which is temporal to that which is eternal. To describe our earthy bodies, it uses the term "earthy house of this tabernacle." A tabernacle is similar to a tent, which is categorized as temporal; it is not a permanent dwelling. By design, tabernacles are fashioned to be taken down at a moment's notice; hence, the association with our mortal bodies as they are fleeting and endure only for a short time. As spirit beings, our fleshly bodies serve as our earthy houses for a specified period of time.

The same contrast that exists between a tabernacle and a building is also true as it relates to the natural and spiritual body. Whereas a tabernacle is temporary, a building is permanent. By comparison, while a tabernacle can be moved in a moment making it temporary, a building is fixed and cannot be moved so easily making it comparatively eternal.

For the believer, death simply represents putting off our temporal houses in exchange for eternal houses, which we will receive at the first resurrection (1 Corinthians Chapter 15). Therefore, death is not the end. As spirit beings, we are eternal, but our houses are temporary.

*As believers in Christ, it is important that we don't confuse who we are with the houses we are in.* If we do that, we will live after the flesh. However, if we understand that we are spirits who are connected to God and one with Him, we will live after the Spirit, which is our higher self. We would live after the true essence of our lives. This is why atheistic and agnostic beliefs that dismiss the existence of God are designed to focus solely on your fleshly, mortal existence and consequently, life after the flesh.

In fact, atheism is not just the lack of belief in God (Yahweh); it also includes the rejection of the existence of any god, supernatural being, or spiritual being. Similar to this, agnosticism is the belief that the existence of God is unknown and, therefore, unknowable. Like one once said to me, "My logical mind does not allow me to grasp the existence of God."

Both of these ideologies reject the notion that humans are spiritual beings. Instead of using the term "soul" or "spirit," words such as "awareness" or "consciousness" are utilized. In general, they subscribe to the idea that once you die, you are gone. In essence, they don't believe in life after death but that at death, your conscious life or existence ends. To this end, the "You only live once," slogan has gained popularity encouraging many to pursue fleshly endeavors. However, as we have already discussed the Bible teaches us a different principle.

To provide a meaningful summary of this discourse on our constitution, Genesis 1:26 conveys that humanity is created in the image and likeness of God. John 4:24 points out that "God is a spirit." This is His very substance. Therefore, when He created humanity, He made us like Him in that we are also spirit beings. Additionally, we are made in His image, which pertains to our human form or shape. God did this because as His sons and representatives on Earth, this provided us with the ability to represent Him and function on His behalf.

When God breathed into Adam the "breath of life," He was transferring His life or His essence into humanity. Hence, like Him, we are also immortal beings. Of note, the same cannot be said for animals in that while they have life, it was not breathed into them by God. If that was done, it would have produced the same spiritual existence or life as human beings. I cannot say with certainty that all dogs (and cats for good measure) go to heaven.

As a principle established by God based on our constitution, He mandated that all spirit beings be clothed in order to function on the earth. Therefore, even though we are in His likeness, He gave us an earthy house. Hence, once the earthy house is dissolved or we die, our spirits go back to God. This tenet disqualifies the notion that after death, spirits or ghosts roam the earth because based on the principle of God and supported by Scripture, this is unlawful. Moreover, God also subjected Himself to the same principle as noted in Hebrews 10:5, which says, "Wherefore when He (Jesus) cometh into the world, He saith, Sacrifice and offering thou wouldest not, but a body has thou prepared me." Hence, God, in compliance with His own law, also came in the fashion of a man. He had to be clothed with an earthy tabernacle to function on the earth.

Furthermore, John 4:24, in recognition that God is a Spirit, continues and says, "And they that worship him must worship him in spirit and in truth." As spirit beings, true worship is when the true essence of who we are (spirit) connects and communes with God as He is a Spirit. Consequently, worship occurs when spirit connects to Spirit in an atmosphere of truth. Worship is an intimate experience of spirits as a result of being one. This is why we have to be cautious of who we connect with.

1 Corinthians 6:16-17 gives the natural example of sexual intercourse to illustrate that the act joins two people and they become one flesh. In using the spiritual parallel, when we are joined to the Lord, we are one spirit with Him.

> 16. What? know ye not that he which is joined to an harlot is one body? for two, saith he, shall be one flesh.
>
> 17. But he that is joined unto the Lord is one spirit. (1 Corinthians 6:16-17)

As a result of Adam's transgression, all humanity became spiritually dead, which is separation from God. However, through belief in Jesus Christ, we are made alive. Consequently, we are reunited with the Father and one spirit with Him.

## WE ARE SPIRIT BEINGS

To be clear, as human beings, we are truly spirits. As previously mentioned, God is a Spirit, and He deposited Himself into us. Therefore, we are made in His likeness (Genesis 1:26). This is the real person inside of us. Job 32:8 says, "But there is a spirit in man: and the inspiration of the Almighty giveth them understanding." When God communicates to us, it is His Spirit connecting with our spirits. The physical body we are in is not the true essence of who we are. Therefore, as far as God is concerned, you are not Asian, Mexican, black, white, fat, slim, male, or female. These are all descriptions that pertain to the houses we are in. They are attached to your identity as a living soul. There are several Scriptures, which express that we are spirits or directly refer to our "inward man" or "inner man."

- Hebrews 12:9 refers to God as <u>the Father of spirits</u>
- Hebrews 12:23 speaks of <u>the spirits of just (righteous) men made perfect</u>
- 2 Corinthians 4:16 says, "For which cause we faint not; but though our outward man perish, yet <u>the inward man</u> is renewed day by day."
- Ephesians 3:16, makes a petition, "That he (God) would grant you, according to the riches of his glory, to be strengthened with might by his Spirit <u>in the inner man</u>."

In John Chapter 3, while having a conversation with Nicodemus, Jesus said to him, "Except a man be born again, he cannot see the kingdom of God." Thinking from a natural perspective, Nicodemus replied, "Can he enter the second time into his mother's womb, and be born?" However, Jesus clarified His statement by saying, "Except a man be born of water and of the Spirit, he cannot enter into the kingdom of God." This was further emphasized with the contrasting statement, "That which is born of flesh is flesh; and that which is born of the Spirit is spirit." Essentially, as we are spirits when we become born again, it is our spirits that are reborn or made alive.

While having a conversation with the Sadducees in Matthew 22:32 and speaking of Abraham, Isaac, and Jacob, Jesus said to them, "God is not the God of the dead but of the living." This statement not only reinforces the eternal nature of our spirits, but it also highlights that at death, it is simply our physical bodies that die, not the true essence of who we are.

The focus of this chapter was to provide an earnest contribution to our constitutional makeup as human beings in order to establish a proper foundation for the discussion of what happens when we die. Of note, there should be a better appreciation for the association of the body, soul, and spirit, as well as a clear distinction between the three.

# Chapter Two

# Those Who Have Fallen Asleep

With a better understanding of our configuration as human beings and clarity concerning the body, soul, and spirit, we can now progress in our discussion of what happens at death. Throughout Scripture, the word "sleep" is often associated with death. Why does the Bible use sleep to illustrate the concept of death? First, the use of sleep as a euphemism for death denotes a state of rest in which you are unconscious of what is transpiring around you. It also speaks of being in a lifeless state. Several scriptural references that use the word "sleep" to indicate death are listed below:

> And when thy days be fulfilled, and thou shalt sleep with thy fathers, I will set up thy seed after thee, which shall proceed out of thy bowels, and I will establish his kingdom. (2 Samuel 7:12)

> And why dost thou not pardon my transgression, and take away mine iniquity? for now shall I sleep in the dust; and thou shalt seek me in the morning, but I shall not be. (Job 7:21)

> Consider and hear me, O LORD my God: lighten mine eyes, lest I sleep the sleep of death. (Psalm 13:3)

52. And the graves were opened; and many bodies of the saints which slept arose,

53. And came out of the graves after his resurrection, and went into the holy city, and appeared unto many. (Matthew 27:52-53)

> These things said he: and after that he saith unto them, Our friend Lazarus sleepeth; but I go, that I may awake him out of sleep. (John 11:11)

13. But I would not have you to be ignorant, brethren, concerning them which are asleep, that ye sorrow not, even as others which have no hope.

14. For if we believe that Jesus died and rose again, even so them also which sleep in Jesus will God bring with him.

15. For this we say unto you by the word of the Lord, that we which are alive and remain unto the coming of the Lord shall not prevent them which are asleep.

16. For the Lord himself shall descend from heaven with a shout, with the voice of the archangel, and with the trump of God: and the dead in Christ shall rise first:

17. Then we which are alive and remain shall be caught up together with them in the clouds, to meet the Lord in the air: and so shall we ever be with the Lord. (1 Thessalonians 4:13-17)

The Bible uses sleep to characterize death because the same way we are awaken out of everyday sleep like a normal occurrence, we will also be awakened from the sleep of death. Not only does this cancel the notion that you only live once, but it also indicates that physical death is not a permanent condition. Rather, it is a state of rest as there will be an awakening from sleep, or in essence, there is life after death. Therefore, the dead are characterized as in a state of sleep awaiting resurrection or to be awakened.

In the example of Lazarus of Bethany in John Chapter 11, notice the terminology used by Jesus even though Lazarus was actually dead. He said Lazarus is asleep, and He is going to wake him (John 11:11). The passage indicates that Lazarus remained in a state of sleep until he was awakened by Jesus.

In the previous chapter, it was determined based on Scripture that the breath of life entering man's nostrils caused him to come alive (Genesis 2:7). Therefore, in reverse, once the breath of life ceases, resulting in death, the body returns to the dust and the spirit returns to God (Ecclesiastes 12:7). Furthermore, according to Scripture, in this state of death (or sleep), consciousness of what is transpiring on Earth also ceases. Moreover, the dead have no share or portion of what occurs on Earth.

> 5. For the living know that they shall die: but the dead know not anything, neither have they any more a reward; for the memory of them is forgotten.
>
> 6. Also their love, and their hatred, and their envy, is now perished; neither have they any more a portion forever in anything that is done under the sun. (Ecclesiastes 9:5-6)

Notice that the passage specifically uses the term "under the sun," which is an indication that as it relates to the goings-on of what transpires on Earth, the dead have no portion in it. Many erroneously use this verse of Scripture to support the notion of "soul sleep." However, this is not what this verse is communicating. This fact will become more evident later in this chapter and also in Chapter 6 during Jesus' account of the rich man and Lazarus.

## RESURRECTION: AWAKENING FROM SLEEP

With the understanding that death is characterized as sleep and there will be an awakening, Jesus says in John 5:28-29:

> 28. Marvel not at this: for the hour is coming, in the which all that are in the graves shall hear his voice,

> 29. And shall come forth; they that have done good, unto the resurrection of life; and they that have done evil, unto the resurrection of damnation.

Believers won't need an immortal body immediately after death because we will not be on Earth but with the Lord. Recall that 2 Corinthians 5:4 refers to this as being "unclothed." We also discussed the principle that spirits require a body to function on Earth. Thus, our bodies need to be resurrected as we will spend eternity on Earth. Therefore, in John 5:28-29, Jesus was referring to the resurrection of our earthly bodies that were sown in the earth. He was speaking of the union of our spirits with our immortal bodies, which we will receive during the first resurrection.

2 Corinthians 5:8 says, "To be absent from the body is to be present with the Lord." Additionally, in Philippians 1:23, Paul expresses a desire to depart or die and to be with Christ. However, it should be noted that prior to Jesus' resurrection, this was not the case for those considered righteous. This will be explained in Chapter 6. The word "present" in 2 Corinthians 5:8 means to be among one's own people or to be home. When the righteous die, they go to be with the Lord. This supports the position that once our spirits leave our bodies, they return to God. This is why 1 Thessalonians 4:14 says during the resurrection, "Them that sleep in Jesus will God bring with Him."

First, the term, "them that sleep in Jesus" signifies those who are born again or who are one with Him and have died. Therefore, when the Lord returns, He will bring "them," the righteous dead with Him. This further validates the position that they are not in the grave in a condition of soul sleep. Hence, during the first resurrection, your spirit that goes to God when you die will connect with the body that was sown in the grave. However, during the first resurrection, that body will be quickened or made immortal (1 Corinthians 15:53-54). Therefore, concerning the discussion of resurrection, the Word of God is very clear that the earthly body of everyone who has died is presently in the grave; this represents a state of sleep. Hence, only your body will be asleep, not your spirit. Upon death, your spirit will be present with the Lord. Again, this nullifies the popular notion of "soul sleep," for our spirits will be with God. However, at the voice of Jesus, there will be a resurrection or an awakening of our bodies from sleep. Those who have done good or the righteous will undergo the resurrection of life, whereas the unrighteous will face the resurrection of damnation referred to as the second death (Revelation 20:14-15). Daniel also echoes this same position in Daniel 12:2:

> And many of them that sleep in the dust of the earth shall awake, some to everlasting life and some to shame and everlasting contempt.

We will discuss the resurrection in greater detail in Chapter 3. However, as we further examine the topic of those who have fallen asleep, the Bible makes us aware that there are a few exceptions to this. There are those who have not tasted death. In particular, Scripture gives the accounts of Enoch and Elijah who were translated that they should not see death. Furthermore, on the same topic, there is also much debate concerning Moses in that even though he died and was buried, his body was never found. Let us take a closer look at these three individuals relative to the discussion of falling asleep.

## Enoch

> 23. And all the days of Enoch were three hundred sixty and five years:

> 24. And Enoch walked with God: and he was not; for God took him. (Genesis 5:23-24)

Hebrews 11:5, which serves as a parallel verse to Genesis 5:23-24, says plainly that Enoch was translated so he should not see death and no one could find him.

> By faith Enoch was translated that he should not see death; and was not found, because God had translated him: for before his translation he had this testimony, that he pleased God (Hebrews 11:5).

The Greek word for translated in Hebrews 11:5 is *metatithēmi*, which means to transfer (move from one place to another) or to change (give up one thing for another). Enoch, therefore, was transferred from one realm to another realm (from the earth to heaven). He was also transformed from one state to another state (changed from moral to immortality). When we combine Genesis 5:23-24 and Hebrews 11:5, we can conclude that God took Enoch that he should *not* see death. Therefore, Enoch did not fall asleep or experience death but was translated. Hence, the discussion concerning the resurrection does not apply to him. Additionally, the same is true concerning Elijah.

# Elijah

> 1. And it came to pass, when the LORD would take up Elijah into heaven by a whirlwind, that Elijah went with Elisha from Gilgal.
>
> 2. And Elijah said unto Elisha, Tarry here, I pray thee; for the LORD hath sent me to Bethel. And Elisha said unto him, As the LORD liveth, and as thy soul liveth, I will not leave thee. So they went down to Bethel.
>
> 3. And the sons of the prophets that were at Bethel came forth to Elisha, and said unto him, Knowest thou that the LORD will

take away thy master from thy head today? And he said, Yea, I know it; hold ye your peace.

4. And Elijah said unto him, Elisha, tarry here, I pray thee; for the LORD hath sent me to Jericho. And he said, As the LORD liveth, and as thy soul liveth, I will not leave thee. So they came to Jericho.

5. And the sons of the prophets that were at Jericho came to Elisha, and said unto him, Knowest thou that the LORD will take away thy master from thy head today? And he answered, Yea, I know it; hold ye your peace.

6. And Elijah said unto him, Tarry, I pray thee, here; for the LORD hath sent me to Jordan. And he said, As the LORD liveth, and as thy soul liveth, I will not leave thee. And they two went on.

7. And fifty men of the sons of the prophets went, and stood to view afar off: and they two stood by Jordan.

8. And Elijah took his mantle, and wrapped it together, and smote the waters, and they were divided hither and thither, so that they two went over on dry ground.

9. And it came to pass, when they were gone over, that Elijah said unto Elisha, Ask what I shall do for thee, before I be taken away from thee. And Elisha said, I pray thee, let a double portion of thy spirit be upon me.

10. And he said, Thou hast asked a hard thing: nevertheless, if thou see me when I am taken from thee, it shall be so unto thee; but if not, it shall not be so.

11. And it came to pass, as they still went on, and talked, that, behold, there appeared a chariot of fire, and horses of fire, and parted them both asunder; and Elijah went up by a whirlwind into heaven.

12. And Elisha saw it, and he cried, My father, my father, the chariot of Israel, and the horsemen thereof. And he saw him no more: and he took hold of his own clothes, and rent them in two pieces (2 Kings 2:1-12).

Consistently throughout the above passage, it is documented that the Lord would take Elijah. As in the case of Enoch, there is a great similarity to Elijah as he was also taken away or translated. The same Hebrew word used to describe how Enoch was translated in Genesis 5:23-24 is also used in 2 Kings 2:1-12 concerning Elijah. The Hebrew word used in both cases is *laqach*, which means to take away, to take up, and to carry off. Hebrews 11:5 describes this as being translated and points to the fact that the activities surrounding both events are similar. Therefore, as with Enoch, Elijah also did not taste death or sleep in the dust of the earth but was translated and changed.

## MOSES

On the other hand, unlike Enoch and Elijah, the Bible actually provides the account of Moses' death.

5. So Moses the servant of the LORD died there in the land of Moab, according to the word of the LORD.

6. And he buried him in a valley in the land of Moab, over against Bethpeor: but no man knoweth of his sepulcher unto this day. (Deuteronomy 34:5-6)

Seeing that the death of Moses is recorded in Scripture, why is he included in the conversation about Enoch and Elijah who clearly did not taste death or fall asleep? The Bible provides many examples of those who died and also includes the details of their burial. However, in the case of Moses, the scenario concerning his death was completely different. In the first instance, as outlined in Deuteronomy 34:5-6, God is actually the one who buried Moses, distinguishing it from other burials. Furthermore, in addition to not knowing where the sepulcher or grave of Moses is, like Enoch and Elijah, his body was never found. In fact, the whereabouts of Moses' body was such a contentious item, that in the book of Jude, the devil disputed with the archangel Michael concerning it. Obviously, the matter pertaining to the body of Moses was one the Lord oversaw Himself.

> Yet Michael the archangel, when contending with the devil he disputed about the body of Moses, durst not bring against him a railing accusation, but said, The Lord rebuke thee. (Jude 1:9)

The Gospels of Matthew, Mark, and Luke furnish us with the account of Jesus' transfiguration. The word "transfigured" is the Greek word *metamorphoo*, which denotes a change in appearance or a transformation to another form. Matthew says that during this transformation, Jesus' face shone like the sun, in that His raiment or clothes was white as light. Luke's description says that the fashion of His countenance was altered, and His raiment was white and glistening (Luke 9:28-31). Mark also provides similar details in Mark 9:2-13. All of the accounts reveal that during this event, both Moses and Elijah appeared alongside Jesus. Luke highlights that the conversation was concerning Jesus' upcoming death. Obviously, for Moses (and Elijah) to appear and talk to Jesus, he could no longer be dead or in a state of sleep. Let us look at Matthew's account of the transfiguration of Jesus Christ.

1. And after six days Jesus taketh Peter, James, and John his brother, and bringeth them up into an high mountain apart,

2. And was transfigured before them: and his face did shine as the sun, and his raiment was white as the light.

3. And, behold, there appeared unto them Moses and Elias talking with him.

4. Then answered Peter, and said unto Jesus, Lord, it is good for us to be here: if thou wilt, let us make here three tabernacles; one for thee, and one for Moses, and one for Elias.

5. While he yet spake, behold, a bright cloud overshadowed them: and behold a voice out of the cloud, which said, This is my beloved Son, in whom I am well pleased; hear ye him.

6. And when the disciples heard it, they fell on their face, and were sore afraid.

7. And Jesus came and touched them, and said, Arise, and be not afraid.

8. And when they had lifted up their eyes, they saw no man, save Jesus only. (Matthew 17:1-8)

With the exception of Enoch, Elijah, and Moses, every other person that has died (obviously excluding Christ) is in a state of sleep awaiting the resurrection of the body. Even Lazarus (John Chapter 11) and the saints who were brought back to life after Jesus' resurrection (Matthew 27:50-53) also later died or fell asleep again and are awaiting the resurrection. There is no indication that Lazarus was brought back to life with a resurrected or immortal body. He was resurrected with the same natural or mortal body he had prior to death. He and the others neither had resurrected bodies nor were they changed from mortal to immortal. In fact, Jesus is the <u>firstfruits</u> of them who sleep (1 Corinthians 15:20). In understanding the resurrection of the dead, the term "firstfruit" is an important principle for consideration. Therefore, it will be explored in detail in the next chapter.

## HAS ANYONE GONE TO HEAVEN?

> And no man hath ascended up to heaven, but he that came down from heaven, even the Son of man which is in heaven. (John 3:13)

If this verse of Scripture is read in isolation, it would give the impression that no one has gone to heaven and would also seem to contradict what we have just discussed. However, Scripture provides sufficient evidence that at the time of the statement, Enoch, Elijah, and Moses had indeed ascended to heaven. Therefore, what is Jesus actually referring to in this passage? Is the subject matter really about ascending to or going to heaven? Absolutely not! As outlined in my book, *The Volume of the Book: Insights into Rightly Dividing the Word of Truth*, the proper context of Scripture must always be maintained even when a single verse of Scripture is under consideration. With that said, to understand this verse, we have to take into account the context of the entire chapter. Moreover, doctrine must not be based on one scripture, but the reconciliation of all scriptures on the subject. This is referred to as the whole of Scripture context.

In John Chapter 3, the main subject is salvation and entrance into the kingdom of God. Throughout the chapter, to explain being born again, Jesus was employing the principle of using earthly things to describe spiritual or heavenly operations (Romans 1:20). For example, to explain salvation, He specifically uses the term "born again," which speaks of rebirth. However, He was specific in contrasting being born after the flesh to being born after the Spirit. Additionally, to describe being born of the Spirit, He uses the illustration of the wind.

Based on this premise of using natural examples, He says in John 3:11 that we can only speak concerning the things we know or are familiar with. Therefore, when speaking to Nicodemus and explaining the process of being born again He used earthly examples with which he was familiar. Jesus took this approach because that is what Nicodemus knew and could relate to. Nevertheless, Nicodemus still did not accept what He was saying. In response, Jesus said in John 3:12, "If while using earthly examples you do not believe me (and you are familiar with these), how will you understand if I try to explain what I am saying in heavenly terms (and you are not familiar with these)?" He was translating heavenly principles into earthy examples for Nicodemus to understand.

To validate His position on being qualified to explain heavenly things, Jesus says in John 3:13, that no man (except for Himself) has ascended into heaven (and returned). Additionally, He adds that He descended from heaven. Essentially, Jesus was saying He was the only one qualified to speak of heavenly things. This is because He is the one who is from heaven and is acquainted with heavenly things. Hence, the statement had nothing to do with who has gone to heaven but simply about being qualified to use earthly principles to explain heavenly ones. In summary, Jesus used earthy illustrations to explain heavenly matters because no other person has gone to heaven and come back to explain these principles. If he had used heavenly examples to convey His message, we would not understand. Therefore, He spoke in an earthly language, so we could understand.

# Chapter Three

# The First and Second Resurrections

## The Awakening from Sleep

To this point, we have discussed the components that make us human beings. They are our earthy bodies and the breath of life or spirit that makes us living souls. In addition, we have also examined the reality of those who have fallen asleep and the awakening that will occur during the resurrection of the dead. In this chapter, we will discuss the resurrection or the wakening from sleep in greater detail. In this respect, it should be noted that the Bible speaks of two resurrections:

1. The resurrection of the righteous
2. The resurrection of the wicked

These take place at separate intervals and are referred to in Scripture as the first and the second resurrections.

## THE FIRST RESURRECTION

1. And I saw an angel come down from heaven, having the key of the bottomless pit and a great chain in his hand.

2. And he laid hold on the dragon, that old serpent, which is the Devil, and Satan, and bound him a thousand years,

3. And cast him into the bottomless pit, and shut him up, and set a seal upon him, that he should deceive the nations no more, till the thousand years should be fulfilled: and after that he must be loosed a little season.

4. And I saw thrones, and they sat upon them, and judgment was given unto them: and I saw the souls of them that were beheaded for the witness of Jesus, and for the word of God, and which had not worshipped the beast, neither his image, neither had received his mark upon their foreheads, or in their hands; and they lived and reigned with Christ a thousand years.

5. But the rest of the dead lived not again until the thousand years were finished. This is **the first resurrection.**

6. Blessed and holy is he that hath part in **the first resurrection**: on such **the second death** hath no power, but they shall be priests of God and of Christ, and shall reign with him a thousand years. (Revelation 20:1-6)

What exactly is the first resurrection compared to the second resurrection? Who are involved in each one? Additionally, Revelation 20:6 also speaks of the second death, which indicates that there is, indeed, the first death. Hence, there is not only a first and second resurrection but also a first and second death. What are the distinctions between the two occurrences? All of these questions will be addressed in this chapter. However, let us first focus our attention on the first resurrection.

13. But I would not have you to be ignorant, brethren, concerning them which are asleep, that ye sorrow not, even as others which have no hope.

14. For if we believe that Jesus died and rose again, even so **them also which sleep in Jesus will God bring with him.**

15. For this we say unto you by the word of the Lord, that we which are alive and remain unto the coming of the Lord shall not prevent them which are asleep.

16. For the Lord himself shall descend from heaven with a shout, with the voice of the archangel, and with the trump of God: and the dead in Christ shall rise first:

17. Then we which are alive and remain shall be caught up together with them in the clouds, to meet the Lord in the air: and so shall we ever be with the Lord.

18. Wherefore comfort one another with these words. (1 Thessalonians 4:13-18)

The above passage is designed to offer comfort, as well as hope to believers, concerning the coming of the Lord. This is often referred to as the rapture and initiates the first resurrection. It targets believers who have fallen asleep (the dead in Christ), as well as believers who will be alive when Christ appears. Furthermore, the passage provides the order in which those involved in the first resurrection (believers) will be taken up. It points out that, at the last trump or trumpet, the dead in Christ will be the first to rise.

It should be noted that even if someone has been cremated, the first law of thermodynamics offers the principle that matter cannot be destroyed, only changed from one form to another. On that note, many people have mixed reactions concerning the subject of cremation. In fact, during a conversation with a group of friends, the question was asked, "Why would someone do that?" While cremation is not my specific preference, it seems that as it pertains to our earthly houses, we sometimes pay more attention to what happens to this temporal tent after we die, than emphasizing the condition of our eternal spirits— the true person. Nevertheless, in whatever form, (cremation or otherwise) upon death, the body goes back to the dust (Ecclesiastes 12:7) and for the most part, this represents the grave.

As we will soon discuss, the Bible uses the natural example of planting a seed and the process of germination to describe how bodies that are planted in the earth (as seeds) will be quickened during the resurrection. As mentioned in the previous chapter, those who have died in Christ are presently with the Lord, and He will bring them with Him during the event outlined in 1 Thessalonians 4:14. However, the dead are currently unclothed or in spirit form. Hence, when they return with the Lord, they will then be clothed with their immortal bodies. These are the bodies of believers that were sown in the earth but as a result of being quickened will be immortal. However, according to 1 Corinthians 15:37, the body that is sown in the ground is not the body that will be resurrected. After the dead in Christ are resurrected, believers who are still alive will be caught up (raptured) together with them to meet the Lord in the air. They will be instantly changed from mortal to immortal. *This entire event can be categorized as a clothing ceremony, where believers put on their eternal house* (2 Corinthians 5:1-4).

There is so much confusion regarding the resurrection of the dead because of a lack of reconciliation of Scripture. This is the same principle as the whole of Scripture context mentioned previously. Recall that this is the practice of examining all Scripture regarding a particular subject and allowing Scripture to interpret Scripture. In this regard, let us revisit the details of the first resurrection. Notice that 1 Thessalonians 4:16 says, "And the dead in Christ shall rise first." Alone, this verse may provide the impression that the dead in Christ are actually in the grave in a state of sleep. This is where many get the incorrect doctrine of soul sleep. However, notice that earlier in the same passage, 1 Thessalonians

4:14 says, "Them which also sleep in Jesus will God bring with Him." To this, we can also reiterate 2 Corinthians 5:8, which says, "To be absent from the body and to be present with the Lord." The logical question would be how can God bring believers with Him if they are also to rise from the grave? Because we have a better understanding of our configuration: body, soul, and spirit, as well as what happens to each part upon death, we now have a better perspective on the resurrection.

As we have discussed, upon death, our eternal spirits go to God, and our bodies go back to the earth. Death is the separation of our spirits from our mortal bodies. Moreover, during the first resurrection, God will bring with Him those that died in Christ. Their mortal bodies that were sown in the ground will then be quickened and united with their spirits. Hence, the dead in Christ will be the first to rise. Furthermore, those who are alive will be caught up in the air and changed from mortal to immortal.

Death = Separation of the spirit from the mortal body.

Resurrection = Reuniting the spirit with an immortal body.

Notice that 1 Thessalonians 4:13-18 provides an overview of the event, which describes the first resurrection. However, 1 Corinthians Chapter 15 offers additional details concerning the subject. In this regard, let us look at 1 Corinthians 15:20-57:

20. But now is Christ risen from the dead, and become the firstfruits of them that slept.

21. For since by man came death, by man came also the resurrection of the dead.

22. For as in Adam all die, even so in Christ shall all be made alive.

23. But every man in his own order: Christ the firstfruits; afterward they that are Christ's at his coming.

24. Then cometh the end, when he shall have delivered up the kingdom to God, even the Father; when he shall have put down all rule and all authority and power.

25. For he must reign, till he hath put all enemies under his feet.

26. The last enemy that shall be destroyed is death.

27. For he hath put all things under his feet. But when he saith, all things are put under him, it is manifest that he is excepted, which did put all things under him.

28. And when all things shall be subdued unto him, then shall the Son also himself be subject unto him that put all things under him, that God may be all in all.

29. Else what shall they do which are baptized for the dead, if the dead rise not at all? why are they then baptized for the dead?

30. And why stand we in jeopardy every hour?

31. I protest by your rejoicing which I have in Christ Jesus our Lord, I die daily.

32. If after the manner of men I have fought with beasts at Ephesus, what advantageth it me, if the dead rise not? let us eat and drink; for tomorrow we die.

33. Be not deceived: evil communications corrupt good manners.

34. Awake to righteousness, and sin not; for some have not the knowledge of God: I speak this to your shame.

35. But some man will say, How are the dead raised up? and with what body do they come?

36. Thou fool, that which thou sowest is not quickened, except it die:

37. And that which thou sowest, thou sowest not that body that shall be, but bare grain, it may chance of wheat, or of some other grain:

38. But God giveth it a body as it hath pleased him, and to every seed his own body.

39. All flesh is not the same flesh: but there is one kind of flesh of men, another flesh of beasts, another of fishes, and another of birds.

40. There are also celestial bodies, and bodies terrestrial: but the glory of the celestial is one, and the glory of the terrestrial is another.

41. There is one glory of the sun, and another glory of the moon, and another glory of the stars: for one star differeth from another star in glory.

42. So also is the resurrection of the dead. It is sown in corruption; it is raised in incorruption:

43. It is sown in dishonour; it is raised in glory: it is sown in weakness; it is raised in power:

44. It is sown a natural body; it is raised a spiritual body. There is a natural body, and there is a spiritual body.

45. And so it is written, The first man Adam was made a living soul; the last Adam was made a quickening spirit.

46. Howbeit that was not first which is spiritual, but that which is natural; and afterward that which is spiritual.

47. The first man is of the earth, earthy: the second man is the Lord from heaven.

48. As is the earthy, such are they also that are earthy: and as is the heavenly, such are they also that are heavenly.

49. And as we have borne the image of the earthy, we shall also bear the image of the heavenly.

50. Now this I say, brethren, that flesh and blood cannot inherit the kingdom of God; neither doth corruption inherit incorruption.

51. Behold, I shew you a mystery; We shall not all sleep, but we shall all be changed,

52. In a moment, in the twinkling of an eye, at the last trump: for the trumpet shall sound, and the dead shall be raised incorruptible, and we shall be changed.

53. For this corruptible must put on incorruption, and this mortal must put on immortality.

54. So when this corruptible shall have put on incorruption, and this mortal shall have put on immortality, then shall be brought to pass the saying that is written, Death is swallowed up in victory.

55. O death, where is thy sting? O grave, where is thy victory?

56. The sting of death is sin; and the strength of sin is the law.

57. But thanks be to God, which giveth us the victory through our Lord Jesus Christ. (1 Corinthians 15:20-57)

Concerning the resurrection of the dead, the above passage begins by establishing the validity of Christ's resurrection. Therefore, before discussing the resurrection of believers, the chapter lays this important foundation. This provides assurance of the resurrection of believers. As a matter of concrete evidence, the chapter gives the account of eyewitnesses who can attest to Christ's resurrection in that He was seen by many after He rose from the dead (1 Corinthians 15:3-8). This reminds me of the narrative that the apostle Peter offers in 2 Peter 1:16 when he says, "What we are telling you is not based on fairy tales or fables but rather, on an eyewitness account." In other words, "I assure you that what I am saying is true because there are eyewitnesses who can substantiate it." In essence, if Jesus did not rise from the dead, our faith would be in vain, and of all men, believers would be the most miserable or pitied (1 Corinthians 15:12-18).

However, with the assurance of Christ's resurrection, the resurrection of believers is also certain. In fact, to support this, 1 Corinthians 15:20 refers to Christ as the firstfruits of them that slept or those that have died. Recall that Hebrews 11:5 says Enoch did not see death. The same can be said of Elijah. Therefore, these accounts do not contradict the statement that Christ is the firstfruits of them which sleep. To understand what is being conveyed in 1 Corinthians 15:20, there has to be an understanding of "firstfruits" as the expression has significance to this discussion.

## FIRSTFRUITS OF THEM WHICH SLEPT

The word "firstfruits" is an agricultural term in which the first sheaf (bundle) of ripe grain from the barley harvest was presented to the Lord in acknowledgment of His blessings. Hence, it was associated with harvest. Additionally, it is connected to the Feast of Firstfruits, which is one of the seven feasts of the Lord outlined in Leviticus Chapter 23. Let us look at Leviticus 23:9-11 for specifics on the Feast:

9. And the LORD spake unto Moses, saying,

10. Speak unto the children of Israel, and say unto them, When ye be come into the land which I give unto you, and shall reap the

> harvest thereof, then ye shall bring a sheaf of the firstfruits of your harvest unto the priest:
>
> 11. And he shall wave the sheaf before the LORD, to be accepted for you: on the morrow after the sabbath the priest shall wave it.

Each of the seven feasts was prophetic in nature and they all find their fulfillment in Jesus Christ with each being fulfilled at an appointed or fixed time or season.

As mentioned in my book, *The Volume of the Book: Insights into Rightly Dividing the Word of Truth*, the first four spring feasts relate to events that have already occurred. As indicated in Leviticus Chapter 23, the Feast of Passover reveals Jesus as the spotless Lamb who was crucified (sacrificed) on the cross. After His death, the Feast of Unleavened Bread was ushered in when He was buried. The sinless unleavened bread of heaven was placed in the grave, thus, fulfilling the Feast.

Three days later, He resurrected from the dead on the Feast of Firstfruits, becoming the firstfruit from the dead. Fifty days after the Feast of Firstfruits, was the Feast of Pentecost where God poured out His Spirit. All of the feasts were fulfilled precisely on the appointed days as specified in Leviticus Chapter 23. The remaining three fall/autumn feasts are connected to the return of Jesus as King and the establishment of the kingdom of God on earth.

There are several references in Scripture that link harvest with resurrection; one such is Matthew 13:24-30. When Jesus resurrected from the grave, He became the firstfruits from the dead or those who slept. He represents the beginning or the first in place, time, order, or rank of those who slept. Indeed, there were others brought back from the dead, for example, Lazarus (John 11:1-44) and the saints who came back to life after Jesus' resurrection (Matthew 27:50-53). However, they all died again and did not have glorified bodies. On the other hand, when Jesus was resurrected, He had a glorified body and the keys of hell and death (Revelation 1:17-19).

Having the keys of hell and death is an indication that He had power or authority over hell (the grave) and death. Jesus displayed this authority when He resurrected from the dead in a state of immortality.

Being raised from the dead in itself is not the manifestation of having the power over death, for throughout Scripture, many have been brought back to life only to die again. However, resurrection and the transformation to immortality where you never die again is the manifestation of having the keys or authority over hell (the grave) and death. With Christ being the firstfruits or the beginning of them that slept, in terms of His resurrection, this is also an indication that more would follow. The first sheaf of the harvest was a representation of the entire harvest. Therefore, at the resurrection, when believers are changed from mortal to immortality, death will be swallowed up in victory and lose its sting, poison, or impulse (1 Corinthians 15:53-56).

## THE RESURRECTED BODY

After tabling the legitimacy of the resurrection in the first portion of 1 Corinthians Chapter 15, the conversation regarding the resurrection gets a bit more specific and two questions are asked in verse 35:

1. How are the dead raised?
2. And with what body do they come?

To provide a practical answer, an example based on nature is presented. The natural body upon death is compared to seed or bare grain planted in the ground. Afterwards, it will be quickened similar to the process of germination. In simple terms, germination is the process where a plant develops from a seed or spore after a period of dormancy (likened to death).

Similarly, the natural body that is planted in the ground (the grave) is not the body that will be resurrected. It only represents the seed. Just as the tree does not resemble the seed that was sown, our resurrected immortal bodies, once quickened, will not resemble the bodies sown in the ground. The word "quickened" is the Greek word *zoopoleo*, which means to make alive, or to cause to live. It is used primarily in reference to raising the dead to life.

Upon resurrection, every seed or body that is planted will be fashioned as it pleases the Lord. He is the one who determines what the resurrected body will look like. This is why 1 John 3:2 says, "Beloved now are we the sons of God, and it doth not yet appear what we shall be: but we know that, when He shall appear, we shall be like Him; for we shall see Him as He is." We do not know exactly what the glorified or immortal body will look like after the process of germination or quickening. However, we are certain that it will look like the Lord's body, for we will see Him as He is.

Furthermore, to enhance our thinking as it pertains to the variety or variations of the resurrected body, 1 Corinthians 15:39 offers a comparative analysis beginning with the different types of flesh. It emphasizes that not all flesh is the same. For instance, there is a distinction between the flesh of man, beasts, birds, and fish. Therefore, despite all having flesh, there is variety. Moreover, 1 Corinthians 15:40 furthers the concept of diversity by highlighting the fact that there are both celestial (heavenly) bodies, as well as terrestrial (earthly) bodies. Along these lines, it says that the glory or the magnificence of the celestial is one and the glory of the terrestrial is another. Therefore, they each have different levels of glory.

While concentrating on the celestial or heavenly bodies such as the sun, moon, and stars, 1 Corinthians 15:41 makes the distinction that they also have varying degrees of glory or splendor. This is evident from the book of Genesis where the sun is cast as the greater light and the moon is classified as the lesser light (Genesis 1:16). Furthermore, as a collection of celestial bodies, each star differs from another star in glory. Hence, each star is original and has a different level of glory.

*The First and Second Resurrections*

Based on the observable universe, astronomers estimate that there are about 300 billion stars in the Milky Way Galaxy alone. It is further estimated that there are about 100 billion galaxies. Therefore, the number of stars is seemingly infinite. By including the stars in the conversation, which is based on an unlimited number, we get a glimpse of the creativity, originality, and imagination of the Father. Just how the dissimilarity of glory exists between the sun, moon, and the innumerable number of stars, so too will be the bodies of the resurrected dead. Each body will have a different degree of glory.

God is not a cookie-cutter Creator! Even in creation, we see the awesomeness of His fingerprint and handiwork. Similarly, each resurrected body will be specifically patterned, custom made, and one of a kind as it pleases Him.

Apart from the distinction in the glory that each resurrected body will uniquely have, there are general attributes that distinguish the two categories of bodies being the natural body and the spiritual body. Generally speaking, the body that is sown upon death is a natural body but the body that will be raised up in the first resurrection will be a spiritual body. In explaining the difference between the natural body and the spiritual or resurrected body, 1 Corinthians 15:42-44 submits a comparison between the two, as seen in the table below.

Table 2

| **BODY SOWN** | **RESURRECTED BODY** |
|---|---|
| Corruption (that which is perishable and subject to decay) | Incorruption (that which is immortal and not susceptible to decay, sickness, and disease) |
| Dishonor (disgrace and ignominy) | Glory (splendor, magnificence, and dignity) |

| Weakness (infirmity, disease, and sickness) | Power (not liable to infirmity, disease, and sickness) |
| --- | --- |
| Natural Body: A body that is sustained by the breath of life. It is a body of flesh and blood. It is one that is subject to appetites and passions. | Spiritual Body: A body that is higher than natural. It is not a body of flesh and blood. It is not subject to appetites and passions. |
| Mortal (subject to death) | Immortal (undying or everlasting) |

In continuing the distinction between a natural body and a spiritual body, 1 Corinthians 15:45-49 offers a comparison between the first Adam and the last Adam. As discussed in Chapter 1, the first Adam is from the garden of Eden and the last Adam is Jesus Christ. The passage submits that one was a being endowed with life and was simply a living soul, whereas the other is a quickening spirit or one who imparts life. He is the source of life. Hence, the natural body or the one that is sown is fashioned after that of the first Adam. It is natural, comprised of the earth, and has an earthy origin. It is a body that is weak, diseased, and subject to decay. On the other hand, the spiritual or resurrected body is fashioned after the last Adam or the Lord from heaven, This body is spiritual and heavenly or has a heavenly origin. Unlike the natural body, this body is not subject to disease or sickness and is immortal. Hence, as we have borne the image of the earthy body given to us by the first Adam, which is natural, we shall also bear the image of the heavenly body that will be given to us by the last Adam and is spiritual.

Before we can inherit the kingdom of God, there has to be a transformation from the image of the earthy to the image of the heavenly. This is because flesh and blood cannot inherit the kingdom of God (1 Corinthians 15:50). To inherit that which is incorruptible, that which is corruptible, or the natural body has to be changed to a spiritual body. The natural body is corruptible in part due to death, decay, sickness, and disease. Therefore, it has to be transformed so that it can be suitable for a kingdom where these do not exist.

The previous chapter focused on believers who have died or have fallen asleep. In reviewing what we discussed, it was understood that the dead in Christ will be the first to rise (1 Thessalonians 4:16) and have immortal or spiritual bodies. Afterward, those in Christ who are alive (1 Thessalonians 4:17) will be caught up together with them (the ones who slept) to meet the Lord in the air.

When it comes to the transformation of believers who are alive at the coming of the Lord, 1 Corinthians 15:51-52 says how this change will occur is unknown as they will experience an instant transformation. We do not know how this will occur; therefore, that remains a mystery. This change of the dead being raised incorruptible and the transformation of those who are alive will take place instantaneously or as Scripture says in a moment in the twinkling of an eye.

## A Blink, A Wink, And A Twinkle

When it comes to the eye, there are three distinct actions: a blink, a wink, and a twinkle. According to Discovery World, a wink is a controlled movement of the eye; its length is determined by the winker. A blink, on the other hand, is a natural and repeated movement of the eye that takes less than half a second. As a child, we would have staring contests to see who could go the longest without blinking. However, light entering the eye, and reflecting as a twinkle happens in about a billionth of a second or the speed of light. In other words, it happens so quickly that there will not be time to make a decision. In applying this principle to our discussion, this is how quickly the transformation from corruptible and mortal (the natural body) to incorruptible and immortal (the spiritual body) will occur. When this change of mortal to immortality takes place, death shall be swallowed up (devoured or destroyed) in victory.

## IN THIS TENT, WE GROAN

In recognition of the fact that we are eternal spirit beings, subjected to a mortal, natural body, 2 Corinthians 5:4 says, "In this tabernacle we groan or sigh for our heavenly eternal body so that mortality might be swallowed up of life." The word "groan" means to make a deep sound, which expresses grief or displeasure. The person that is groaning is your spirit, which is housed in a temporary earthy house but has a longing desire to be clothed in your heavenly or spiritual house.

Romans 8:18-25 supports this perspective and says:

18. For I reckon that the sufferings of this present time are not worthy to be compared with the glory which shall be revealed in us.

19. For the earnest expectation of the creature waiteth for the manifestation of the sons of God.

20. For the creature was made subject to vanity, not willingly, but by reason of him who hath subjected the same in hope,

21. Because the creature itself also shall be delivered from the bondage of corruption into the glorious liberty of the children of God.

22. For we know that the whole creation groaneth and travaileth in pain together until now.

23. And not only they, but ourselves also, which have the firstfruits of the Spirit, even we ourselves groan within ourselves, waiting for the adoption, to wit, the redemption of our body.

24. For we are saved by hope: but hope that is seen is not hope: for what a man seeth, why doth he yet hope for?

25. But if we hope for that we see not, then do we with patience wait for it.

Beginning at verse 18, the passage by careful consideration makes an evaluation that offers comfort and assurance. It says that when the sufferings (persecutions and afflictions) that we are presently going through are compared to the glory or splendor of our immortal bodies, it is not a worthy comparison. In other words, they are not of corresponding value. In fact, 2 Corinthians 4:17 refers to our present sufferings as light afflictions that last for a moment but work for us a far more exceeding and eternal weight of glory.

In continuing the discussion, Romans 8:19 says that as it pertains to the glory that shall be revealed in us, believers have an anxious and persistent expectation. There is intense anxiety for the unveiling of the sons of God in our glorified bodies. Romans 8:20 then goes on to explain why this longing desire exists. It says the new creation, or the spirit man was subjected to vanity or a natural body. By virtue of the Holy Spirit adopting us (Romans 8:15-17), we are already the sons of God. However, the manifestation of the sons of God spoken of in this chapter represents our full disclosure as sons of God when mortal shall put on immortality, and we are seen in our full glory (1 John 3:1).

Even though we are already the sons of God, at present, we are subjected to vanity, which is a corruptible earthy tabernacle. This is not what we really want; this is not our choice, but for the time, God has subjected or appointed us to this (Romans 8:20-21). However, we know something better, and eternal awaits us, and this infuses us with hope. For we know that we shall be delivered from this earthy, dishonorable bondage of corruption, which is our natural fleshly bodies, into the glorious liberty of the children of God. In other words, as stated in Philippians 3:21, "He shall change our vile bodies, that they may be fashioned like unto his glorious body."

Furthermore, every living creature or the aggregate of things created is groaning and travailing for the adoption or the redemption of our bodies. All of creation is in pain and agony awaiting the change of our bodies from corruption to incorruption. Everything in nature with great expectation is looking with bated breath to see what the sons of God will look like. All of creation stands united, having the same eagerness, coded desire, and expectation. Additionally, the sons of God who have the Spirit of God in them are also groaning for the very same thing.

As a guarantee of the spiritual or incorruptible body, which God has predetermined for us, He has also given us <u>the earnest of His Spirit (2 Corinthians 1:22, Ephesians 1:13-14)</u>. Not only has He given us His Spirit to empower and guide us while we are here on Earth, but it also serves as a deposit or assurance in relation to the redemption of our bodies.

The word "earnest" is the Greek word *arrabon*, which refers to money or a portion of the price given as a down payment. This serves as a promise that the full amount will subsequently be paid, and the purchased possession will be redeemed. Therefore, the Lord gave us His Holy Spirit as a pledge that He will complete the transaction and transform our bodies from mortal to immortal. As a result of having this guarantee, we are infused with confidence. However, despite this confidence, we would rather be absent from the body and present with the Lord. Nevertheless, the key is whether we are present with the Lord (unclothed) or absent from Him (in this body), we labor to be accepted by Him. This is the hope, the redemption of our bodies that causes us to purify ourselves even as He is pure (1 John 3:3).

## THE SECOND RESURRECTION

Now that we have discussed the first resurrection, let us turn our attention to the second resurrection. However, let us first highlight several Scriptures, which specifically emphasize that there are, indeed, two occurrences relative to the resurrection.

> And having hope toward God, which they themselves also allow, that there shall be a resurrection of the dead, both of the just and the unjust. (Acts 24:15)
>
> And many of them that sleep in the dust of the earth shall awake, some to everlasting life, and some to shame and everlasting contempt. (Daniel 12:2)
>
> 28. Marvel not at this: for the hour is coming, in the which all that are in the graves shall hear his voice,
>
> 29. And shall come forth; they that have done good, unto the resurrection of life; and they that have done evil, unto the resurrection of damnation. (John 5:28-29)

Based on the above scriptures, the Bible states that there is a resurrection of the just (righteous), as well as a resurrection of the unjust (unrighteous), each with contrasting rewards. In reference to the first resurrection recall that 1 Thessalonians 4:16-17 acknowledges that the righteous are the only ones involved in this awakening. Therefore, the unrighteous are the ones associated with the second resurrection.

As the day is distinct from the night, so are the first and second resurrections completely different from each other. While one is a resurrection of glory and honor, the other is of damnation and shame. Unfortunately, the great anticipation and glory associated with the first resurrection, which is the resurrection of the just, does not exist for those involved in the second resurrection. Having already provided the perspective of the first resurrection, what exactly are the circumstances surrounding the second resurrection, and what happens after this awakening from sleep?

Before we get into the specific details concerning the second resurrection, the first objective is to establish the timeframe, which occurs between the two resurrections. Not only are they dissimilar in nature and rewards, but they also differ in when they occur. In plain language, Scripture states that the timespan between the first resurrection and the second resurrection is a period of one thousand years.

The righteous who are involved in the first resurrection will reign **on Earth** with Christ for a thousand-year period, which is referred to as the millennium reign of Christ. During this time, Satan will be bound in the bottomless pit, which will prevent him from deceiving the nations of the Earth. At the end of the millennium reign or period of one thousand years, the second resurrection occurs.

> 4. And I saw thrones, and they sat upon them, and judgment was given unto them: and I saw the souls of them that were beheaded for the witness of Jesus, and for the word of God, and which had not worshipped the beast, neither his image, neither had received his mark upon their foreheads, or in their hands; and they lived and reigned with Christ a thousand years.
>
> 5. *But the rest of the dead lived not again until the thousand years were finished. This is the first resurrection.*
>
> 6. Blessed and holy is he that hath part in the first resurrection: on such the second death hath no power, but they shall be priests of God and of Christ, and shall reign with him a thousand years. (Revelation 20:4-6)

Recall that 1 Corinthians 15:54-55, in addressing the transformation of the first resurrection, speaks of the change from corruptible to incorruptible or mortal to immortality. Those undergoing this change will no longer be subjected to the grave, death, or the sting of death. Having already been awakened from the first sleep or the first death, they will no longer face death again or the second death. However, those involved in the second resurrection having already experienced the first death, which is mortal death will also be subjected to the second death.

After the thousand years are completed, Satan will be loosed from his prison for a season. He will deceive the nations, and gather them to do battle against the Lord. However, God will send down fire from heaven and devour them. Also, Satan will be cast into the lake of fire and brimstone to be tormented forever and ever (Revelation 20:7-10).

After these events, those involved in the second resurrection appear before the great white throne for judgment according to their works. Whosoever is not found written in the book of life will be cast into the lake of fire. The second death, therefore, is the judgment for those whose names are not found in the book of life. It should be noted that at present, the spirits of the unrighteous dead are *not* currently in the lake of fire as this represents eternal and final judgment. However, they are in hell, which is a temporary holding place of torment awaiting the second resurrection. This will be discussed at length in Chapter 6.

11. And I saw a great white throne, and him that sat on it, from whose face the earth and the heaven fled away; and there was found no place for them.

12. And I saw the dead, small and great, stand before God; and the books were opened: and another book was opened, which is the book of life: and the dead were judged out of those things which were written in the books, according to their works.

13. And the sea gave up the dead which were in it; and death and hell delivered up the dead which were in them: and they were judged every man according to their works.

14. And death and hell were cast into the lake of fire. *This is the second death.*

15. And whosoever was not found written in the book of life was cast into the lake of fire. (Revelation 20:11-15)

The first death is the mortal death that we have all been appointed to (Hebrews 9:27). However, the second death is reserved for the unrighteous. Whereas the first death is temporary and categorized as sleep, the second death is one of eternal damnation. Notice that there is a direct correlation between the first resurrection and the first death and the second resurrection and the second death. The second death has no power over those involved in the first resurrection. Based on what we have covered in this chapter, the comparison table below highlights the distinction between the first and second resurrection.

Table 3

| FIRST RESURRECTION | SECOND RESURRECTION |
| --- | --- |
| The resurrection of the righteous | The resurrection of the unrighteous |
| Everlasting life | Everlasting contempt and shame |
| The resurrection of life | The resurrection of damnation |
| The Lord shall descend from heaven with a shout with the voice of the archangel and with a trumpet | No descending, no shout, no trumpet |
| Dead in Christ are the first to rise. Those that are alive will be caught up in the air to be with the Lord | Death and hell deliver up the dead which are in them. The dead, small and great stand before God and are judged |
| The resurrection is one of incorruption, immortality, glory, power —a spiritual body | The resurrection of shame and no glory |
| Death has no sting and the grave has no victory | The second death, cast into the lake of fire |

## Christ's Resurrection and His Body

The discussion of resurrection is not complete unless we address the subject of Christ's resurrection. Relative to this, it is important to examine and understand the type of body Jesus resurrected with and its significance. After His resurrection, Mary Magdalene, Joanna, Mary (mother of James), and several other women went to the tomb of Jesus. They realized His body was no longer there.

Afterward, two angels appeared and said to them, "Why seek ye the living among the dead? He is not here, but is risen." The angels then reminded them that Jesus foretold of His resurrection. Therefore, the women went and told the apostles what transpired. However, they did not believe them but considered their words as idle tales. Simply put, they did not believe the account of the women (Luke 24:1-11). Subsequently, Peter ran to the sepulcher and saw the linen Jesus was wrapped in; he wondered what had happened.

After these events, Jesus appeared to Cleopas along with another disciple while they were on the road to Emmaus. While they were speaking to each other, Jesus approached them and asked them what they were talking about and why they were sad. At the time, they were unaware of who He was. Therefore, based on His questions, they relayed to Him the account of Jesus' death and how they were hoping He would have been the one to redeem Israel. Additionally, they recited the account they heard from the women concerning Jesus' empty tomb and the statement from the angels that He was indeed alive.

Notice two things from the passage. First, Cleopas and the other disciple reiterated that they were astonished or surprised by what the women said. Additionally, they stated that when certain disciples went to the tomb, based on what the women said, they did not see Jesus (Luke 24:13-24). Not only were they in disbelief, but they also could not attest to the resurrection for themselves. Based on what they said Jesus chided them and said in Luke 24:25-27:

> 25. O fools, and slow of heart to believe all that the prophets have spoken:
>
> 26. Ought not Christ to have suffered these things, and to enter into his glory?
>
> 27. And beginning at Moses and all the prophets, he expounded unto them in all the scriptures the things concerning himself.

At this point, they still did not know who He was. When they got to the village, they asked Him to stay, and as they ate, their eyes were opened. They finally realized it was Jesus, and He vanished from them. After this experience, they had empirical evidence that He had risen. Hence, they ran and told the eleven apostles what happened (Luke 24:28-35). As Cleopas and the other disciple were relaying the account to the apostles, Jesus appeared to them. Let us look at the narrative in Luke 24:36-43. A similar account is offered in John 20:19-21.

> 36. And as they thus spake, Jesus himself stood in the midst of them, and saith unto them, Peace be unto you.
>
> 37. But they were terrified and affrighted, and supposed that they had seen a spirit.
>
> 38. And he said unto them, Why are ye troubled? and why do thoughts arise in your hearts?
>
> 39. Behold my hands and my feet, that it is I myself: handle me, and see; for a spirit hath not flesh and bones, as ye see me have.
>
> 40. And when he had thus spoken, he shewed them his hands and his feet.
>
> 41. And while they yet believed not for joy, and wondered, he said unto them, Have ye here any meat?

42. And they gave him a piece of a broiled fish, and of an honeycomb.

43. And he took it, and did eat before them. (Luke 24:36-43)

Now, that we have discussed the details surrounding Jesus' resurrection, let us get to the heart of the matter relative to His body. When He appeared to His disciples, they were afraid, thinking that they had seen a spirit. However, to reassure them He was not a spirit, He showed them His hands and feet and said, "Touch me for a spirit doesn't have flesh and bones as I have." Jesus also ate with them. Note, that Jesus invited them to touch Him as proof that He was not a spirit.

As a point of reference, immediately after His resurrection, Jesus could not be touched as He had not yet ascended to the Father in heaven (John 20:17). Immediately after His resurrection, His role changed from that of a sacrificial lamb to High Priest. According to the pattern laid out in the Law, the High Priest went into the Most Holy Place and sprinkled the blood of bulls and goats on the mercy seat for his own sins and for the sins of the people. Therefore, Christ, becoming a High Priest and following the same pattern, took His own blood to the tabernacle in heaven and sprinkled it on the mercy seat, thereby obtaining eternal redemption for humanity (Hebrews 9:11-14). However, unlike the high priest under the law, Jesus did not have to offer a sacrifice for Himself. Nevertheless, after He had performed His responsibilities as High Priest, He could then return to Earth and be touched.

The Scripture says that Jesus is the firstfruit of them who sleep or the first to be resurrected with a glorified body (1 Corinthians 15:20). However, the question is, did Jesus' resurrected body represent a typical glorified body? Even though the resurrected bodies will resemble the type of body Jesus had, I contend that there will be a distinction. Recall that as it pertains to our glorified bodies, 1 John 3:2 says, "Beloved, now are we the sons of God, and it doth not yet appear what we shall be: but we know that, when he shall appear, we shall be like him; for we shall see him as he is." Hence, our precise appearance is unknown.

However, to convince everyone of His resurrection, Jesus had to appear in the form and fashion that everyone was familiar with even though in a glorified body. If He had not appeared as they remembered Him, there would not be a conviction or proof of His resurrection. Recall that when the women told the disciples Jesus had resurrected, they summed it up as idle tales. Therefore, He had to provide substantive evidence that He had, indeed, resurrected. Along these lines, He even showed them His hands and feet (Luke 24:40).

Acts 1:1-3 says that after His resurrection, Jesus showed Himself alive by many fallible (dependable) proofs and was seen of them for a period of forty days while He taught concerning the kingdom of God.

1. The former treatise have I made, O Theophilus, of all that Jesus began both to do and teach,

2. Until the day in which he was taken up, after that he through the Holy Ghost had given commandments unto the apostles whom he had chosen:

3. To whom also he shewed himself alive after his passion by many infallible proofs, being seen of them forty days, and speaking of the things pertaining to the kingdom of God. (Acts 1:1-3)

Jesus needed to be seen in a familiar image as proof of His resurrection, for His resurrection is the cornerstone of our faith and hope. 1 Corinthians 15:1-21, while validating His resurrection, says that many eyewitnesses could attest to it. He was seen of Peter, the disciples, five hundred brethren at one time, James, the apostles, and also Paul. If He did not rise from the dead, our preaching would be in vain. We would have no hope of resurrection, and our faith would also be in vain. Moreover, we would still be in our sins, and of all men, we would be most miserable. However, because of the infallible evidence that He did rise from the dead, we have great assurance of our resurrection, as well as our eternal redemption and inheritance.

## The First and Second Resurrections

After Jesus ascended into heaven the second time and thereafter appeared to John while on the Isle of Patmos, He had a different image and degree of glory. This image of His glorified body was very different from the one He had when He was resurrected. But bear in mind, the purpose was also different.

> 12. And I turned to see the voice that spake with me. And being turned, I saw seven golden candlesticks;
>
> 13. And in the midst of the seven candlesticks one like unto the Son of man, clothed with a garment down to the foot, and girt about the paps with a golden girdle.
>
> 14. His head and his hairs were white like wool, as white as snow; and his eyes were as a flame of fire;
>
> 15. And his feet like unto fine brass, as if they burned in a furnace; and his voice as the sound of many waters.
>
> 16. And he had in his right hand seven stars: and out of his mouth went a sharp two-edged sword: and his countenance was as the sun shineth in his strength.
>
> 17. And when I saw him, I fell at his feet as dead. And he laid his right hand upon me, saying unto me, Fear not; I am the first and the last:
>
> 18. I am he that liveth, and was dead; and, behold, I am alive for evermore, Amen; and have the keys of hell and of death. (Revelation 1:12-18)

Therefore, I contend that our resurrected bodies will be fashioned more like His true glorified body as opposed to the one He had after His resurrection. We shall be like Him for we shall see Him as He is. Additionally, Philippians 3:21 says He shall change our vile bodies or those of low estate that they may resemble His glorious body. Furthermore, our bodies will have varying degrees of glory as stated in 1 Corinthians 15:35-49.

Chapter Four

# I Go To Prepare A Place For You

Now that the first and second resurrections have been addressed, our next topic pertains to the eternal destination of resurrected believers. On this point, it is necessary to discuss the subject of mansions in heaven.

Let's face it, we all have fantasies about our ideal dream home which, when compared to the specifications of others, can be somewhat subjective. Certainly, we envision the layout of the house: something spacious, perhaps a flower garden in the front with a picket fence and a pool in the back. We can see ourselves there, and the reality of achieving this dream can serve as a driving force for attaining it one day. Unfortunately, for many, the ideal dream home remains a fantasy, and the settlement for something "comfortable" is eventually agreed upon. Then we hear that there are mansions in heaven being prepared for believers and the dream of better accommodations stirs within us. In fact, by comparison, the thought of a heavenly mansion far surpasses the notion of anything Earth could possibly offer.

On the subject of mansions in heaven, John Chapter 14 is certainly one of the more popular passages of Scripture used to infuse excitement and hope, not only for believers who have fallen asleep but also for us who are alive. In fact, concerning the highpoint of the text, which is purportedly mansions in heaven prepared for the saints, several songs exist, and elaborate sermons have been preached that often give us goosebumps. Furthermore, there are countless anecdotes of persons who have allegedly had visions of heaven. They have even provided detailed illustrations of the mansions that are reported to be there.

Without directly questioning the authenticity of the visions or the inspiration that drives the songs or sermons, it is always best to examine what Scripture has to say and allow the Bible to interpret itself. In that vein, there are several fundamental questions surrounding John Chapter 14, which have to be answered. It is only through answering these questions that we will have a proper perspective of the message being conveyed and obtain clarity concerning the subject of mansions. The questions are as follows:

1. What is the proper context and perspective of the passage?

2. Throughout the Bible, what is referred to as, "The Father's house?"

3. In the context of the passage, what are mansions?

4. What did Jesus mean when He said, "I go to prepare a place for you"?

5. What did Jesus mean when He said, "I will come again and receive you unto myself that where I am you may be also?"

6. Where are believers going to spend eternity?

# 1. WHAT IS THE CONTEXT AND PERSPECTIVE OF THE PASSAGE?

By far, the Word of God is the final authority on any subject matter. It is the standard by which everything that we believe should be measured. Despite what we hear, be it a song, sermon, or personal anecdote, we have a "more sure" word of prophecy by which to measure everything (2 Peter 1:19). As a premise, the principles of rightly dividing the Word of Truth (2 Timothy 2:15) always have to be employed when studying a verse of Scripture, a passage of Scripture, a complete book of the Bible, or even an entire Testament. Furthermore, the context of Scripture and perspective of Scripture must also be maintained for the true intent of Scripture to be known.

For more insight into these principles, see my book, *The Volume of the Book: Insights into Rightly Dividing the Word of Truth*. In this regard, John Chapter 14 is entrenched in a passage context, which revolves around the discussion of Jesus' death and what was to follow. Additionally, the central theme of the book of John depicts the relationship between the Father and the Son. In that vein, it serves as the blueprint for the relationship between the Father and the sons who would be produced through Christ as He is the firstborn of many brethren (Romans 8:29).

The Gospel of John is one of relationship: Father-son relationship. In fact, you cannot understand the concept of sonship without understanding the Gospel of John. The book gives us insight on how to function as sons in relation to the Father. These two important points provide the framework for understanding John Chapter 14, as well as the entire Gospel of John.

With John Chapter 14 being a part of what is referred to as a passage context, it cannot be read in isolation apart from the other verses or chapters that make up the passage context. In short, a passage context includes all the verses and chapters of a particular book that focus on a specific subject. In this instance, the passage context regarding mansions actually begins in John Chapter 11 and extends to John Chapter 17. However, we will begin the discussion at John Chapter 13.

31. Therefore, when he was gone out, Jesus said, Now is the Son of man glorified, and God is glorified in him.

32. If God be glorified in him, God shall also glorify him in himself, and shall straightway glorify him.

33. Little children, yet a little while I am with you. Ye shall seek me: and as I said unto the Jews, Whither I go, ye cannot come; so now I say to you.

34. A new commandment I give unto you, That ye love one another; as I have loved you, that ye also love one another.

35. By this shall all men know that ye are my disciples, if ye have love one to another.

36. Simon Peter said unto him, Lord, whither goest thou? Jesus answered him, Whither I go, thou canst not follow me now; but thou shalt follow me afterwards.

37. Peter said unto him, Lord, why cannot I follow thee now? I will lay down my life for thy sake.

38. Jesus answered him, Wilt thou lay down thy life for my sake? Verily, verily, I say unto thee, The cock shall not crow, till thou hast denied me thrice. (John 13:31-38)

In John 13:31-32, Jesus foretells of His betrayal and the glorification associated with His death. This is followed by the statement in John 13:36, where He says to Peter, "Whither I go, thou canst not follow me now; but thou shall follow me afterwards." In speaking of His death, Jesus said to Peter, "You cannot follow me now." However, knowing what would be accomplished through His death, He continues, "But you shall follow me afterwards." The place where they would follow Him is revealed in the context of John Chapter 14.

Jesus was saying, "To follow me, I first have to prepare a place for you and this can only be accomplished if I go away or if I die." Based on this, Thomas then asks a pivotal question in John 14:5. He says to Jesus, if we do not know where you are going, how can we know the way? Jesus then says to him in John 14:6, "I am the way, the truth and the life, no man cometh unto the Father but by me." *Therefore, Jesus was actually speaking about relationship and fellowship with the Father.* In other words, Jesus was saying, "Through death, I am providing you access to the Father." Hence, the entire conversation was simply a message of relationship and unity with the Father.

To have a better appreciation for the type of relationship Jesus was referring to, let us take a few steps back to the beginning of the Gospel of John. In John Chapter 1, the foundation is laid concerning the relationship between the Father and the Son. From the onset of the book, it is evident that Jesus enjoyed unity and oneness with the Father; therefore, He was able to testify of Him.

> No man hath seen God at any time; the only begotten Son, which is in the bosom of the Father, he hath declared him. (John 1:18)

This verse says that no man has seen God at any time. This is not referring to visible manifestations of God for Moses saw the back parts of God (Exodus 33:20-23). Rather, the verse applies to an intimate knowledge of who He truly is. Therefore, it is saying that no man was able to bear witness of God's character. However, He that is in the bosom of the Father (Jesus) can manifest the character of God or be a witness of Him to humanity. He provides a visible manifestation of the Father's nature, and we can trust His testimony because He is the only begotten of the Father.

The Greek word for "only begotten" is *monogenes*, meaning the only one of the family or the only one of the same stock in the relationship of the Father to the Son. Therefore, to provide the best witness possible of who the Father is, He sent His Son. He sent the One who is from His very bosom, which designates a place of closeness or intimacy. As John explains, "The Word was made flesh and dwelt among us and we beheld His glory as the only begotten of the Father" (John 1:14). The very character of God took on flesh in order for humanity to see who He truly is.

In John 14:9, Philip said to Jesus, "Show us the Father." Jesus answered and said, "Have I been so long time with you, and yet hast thou not known me, Philip? He that hath seen me hath seen the Father." In other words, I am a witness of who He is, I am the manifestation of His character…the Father and I are one.

Jesus displayed a Father-Son relationship with God that no one else had previously enjoyed or witnessed. As no one hath seen God, He was able to declare the character of the Father to us. However, not only did Jesus reveal the Father's character to humanity, but He also exemplified the relationship between the Father and the Son. It is important to understand that the concept of sonship did not exist before Christ came. The house that Moses was a part of (Israel) consisted of servants, whereas the house of Christ comprises of sons (Hebrews 3:1-6). Despite Moses' faithfulness, Hebrews 3:5-6 says that he was a servant, whereas Christ is a Son.

The distinction between a servant and a son is poles apart. A servant holds an entirely different position than that of a son with the hallmark being a <u>relationship</u>. For example, servants are not privy to what the master is doing but sons are (John 15:15). Also, inheritance is ordained for sons as opposed to servants (Genesis 15:3-4, Galatians 4:7). Servants have limited access and do not abide in the house forever; their place is not certain. However, sons abide forever, and their places are guaranteed (John 8:36). Servants are subjected to bondage, whereas sons live in freedom and liberty (Galatians 4:21-31). Servants are guided by rules, while sons are directed by relationship (John 5:19).

The Law could only produce servants, whereas Christ can produce sons (Galatians 4:5-6). For more on the significance of being a son, please see my book *God's Eternal Purpose Volume 1:The Establishment of God's Kingdom*.

The purpose of Jesus dying was to expand the Father's house or family with sons. Jesus was the only begotten of the Father; He was the only one in the family but through His death, He would beget more sons into the Father's house and thereby enlarge the family (Hebrews 2:10-13). To get brethren, He had to die for our sins so that we could be reconciled to the Father. He made us one with the Father; thus, creating a Father-son relationship. Moreover, He provided the blueprint of how sons ought to behave in relation to the Father. Now that we have a better understanding of the context and perspective of John Chapter 14, we are better equipped to address the other questions.

## 2. WHAT IS THE FATHER'S HOUSE?

1. Let not your heart be troubled: ye believe in God, believe also in me.

2. In my Father's house are many mansions: if it were not so, I would have told you. I go to prepare a place for you.

3. And if I go and prepare a place for you, I will come again, and receive you unto myself; that where I am, there ye may be also. (John14:1-3)

In addition to the passage context, to understand John Chapter 14, it is imperative to also understand what is meant by the term "the Father's house." Once we determine what this phrase refers to, this establishes the parameters for the entire chapter. The Greek word for "house" in

John 14:2 is *oikia*, which means residence or household. It also means the inhabitants of a house, which points to a family. Therefore, in the context of John 14:2 when Jesus used the term "My Father's house," He was referring to His Father's family or household. Hence, Jesus was saying that within my Father's household or family, there are many places for you to dwell. However, as we have determined from the previous section, dwelling in the house is specifically reserved for sons. Thus, the reason Jesus gave His life for humanity is so we could become the sons of God. Those who believe in Him become members of the Father's family. During this entire conversation, Jesus was essentially promoting access into the family of God.

Based on the predominant interpretation of John 14:2, the Father's house is incorrectly associated with heaven. Unfortunately, this then changes the perspective of the chapter leading to the conclusion of mansions in heaven. However, throughout the Bible, God's house or the Father's house is <u>never</u> referred to as heaven. According to Scripture, the house of God is identified as three distinct things. They are the tabernacle of Moses (Exodus 25:8-9), the temple (Isaiah 56:7, Psalm 27:4, Psalm 84:10, Psalm 93:5, Matthew 21:13), and His sons or body of believers (1 Corinthians 6:19). The tabernacle and temple were for God to dwell among His people, but this was obviously one-sided. It only allowed God to dwell among His people, but they could not dwell in Him, which would create a more perfect dwelling. Hence, God was making it possible for His people (sons) to dwell in Him and He in them. Therefore, He sent Jesus to provide the perfect example of what it means to be begotten of the Father and to dwell in the Father. After we become born again by the Father's incorruptible seed (1 Peter 1:23), we become sons and members of His family or house. We also simultaneously become the habitation or dwelling place of God through the Spirit (Ephesians 2:22, 1 Corinthians 6:19).

Notice that once the proper context of "the Father's house" is presented, then the perspective of the chapter also changes. As Jesus was the only begotten of the Father and a representative of the Father's house, He was charged with expanding the Father's house or family. This was only possible through His death.

## 3. Based on the Context of the Passage, What are Mansions?

In addition to the misconceptions that surround the term "the Father's house," there is also a misunderstanding regarding the word "mansions." Unfortunately, as noted at the beginning of this chapter, the concept of mansions has been measured and fueled by our own desires. Nevertheless, now that we have the proper context concerning the Father's house, this then contributes to a better understanding of mansions. The word "mansions" is the Greek word *mone*, which means the following:

- Habitation
- Abode
- A staying (residence)
- Abiding
- A dwelling (the Holy Spirit dwelling inside believers and believers dwelling in the Father)

While responding to Judas (not Iscariot) in John 14:23, Jesus said, "If a man love me, he will keep my words: and my Father will love him, and we will come unto him, and make our abode with him." The word "abode" in John 14:23 is the same Greek word for mansions in John 14:2. Ironically, in the verses leading up to this one, Jesus actually explains how He and the Father will make their abode with us. Hence, He thoroughly explains the concept of mansions.

> 16. And I will pray the Father, and he shall give you another Comforter, that he may abide with you for ever;
>
> 17. Even the Spirit of truth; whom the world cannot receive, because it seeth him not, neither knoweth him: but ye know him; for he dwelleth with you, and shall be in you.

18. I will not leave you comfortless: I will come to you.

19. Yet a little while, and the world seeth me no more; but ye see me: because I live, ye shall live also.

20. At that day ye shall know that I am in my Father, and ye in me, and I in you. (John 14:16-20)

The Holy Spirit dwelling in us results in us dwelling in the Father and in Christ. This explains how believers can make their abode with the Father and Christ. It is the same experience Jesus was referring to when He used the word "mansions" in John 14:2. In explaining the concept of mansions or making our abode with the Father, Jesus says when you receive the Holy Spirit, you will know that I am in the Father, ye in Me, and I in you.

When Jesus said in John 13:36 that where He was going we would follow Him, He was referring to us dwelling in the Father and being one with the Father as He is. Hence, to explain the notion of dwelling in the Father and the Father dwelling in us, He figuratively uses the word mansions. He was simply using an earthly example of a dwelling place to explain a spiritual operation of dwelling in the Father and the Father dwelling in us.

After foretelling His death and going away, the disciples were troubled. Therefore, to comfort them and explain how they would follow Him, Jesus said in John 14:1, "Let not your hearts be troubled, ye believe in God, believe also in me." In other words, there is no difference between me and the Father. He and I are one. I dwell in Him, and He dwells in Me. I am leaving (dying) so that this same dwelling privilege can be experienced by you as well. Do not be troubled, in my Father's house or in my family are many mansions; there is room for everyone to dwell. However, because this dwelling can only be experienced by sons, Jesus had to give His life.

# 4. I Go to Prepare a Place for You

I am sure by now you realize the ripple effect of having the proper context of Scripture. Because we have established the proper context of John Chapter 14, followed by what is meant by the Father's house and mansions, the phrase, "I go to prepare a place for you," certainly has a different connotation. As we have determined based on the context of the passage, when Jesus said, "I go to prepare a place for you," He was speaking of what would be accomplished through His death. On the contrary, the incorrect context of this verse gives the perspective that Jesus was going to heaven to start a building project. However, the place that He was going to prepare was the ability and privilege of the Father abiding in us, and we in Him.

Jesus' death and resurrection made it possible for humanity to become sons of God or members of the Father's family. Additionally, as a result of His death and the indwelling of the Holy Spirit, this made it possible for the Father to dwell in us and for us to dwell in the Father. This was the nature of His preparations.

As we have explained, this place that He was going to prepare was not in reference to some futuristic hope or elaborate building in heaven. Rather, it is the present experience of being members of the Father's family, dwelling in Him and He in us. Based on the context of John Chapter 14, it is clear that access to the Father and His family is only through Jesus. He is the way, the truth, and the life. It was through death that He provided a way for us to be incorporated into the Father's house.

Throughout John Chapter 14, Jesus highlights the relationship between Him and the Father. He speaks of oneness between them. He speaks of being in the Father and the Father being in Him, which signifies unity dwelling (John 14:10-11). Therefore, by this statement, He was simply promoting the same relationship He enjoyed.

# 5. I Will Come Again and Receive You unto Myself

In John 14:3, Jesus said, "And if I go and prepare a place for you, I will come again, and receive you unto myself; that where I am, there ye may be also." Again, because we have established the proper context of the passage, it should be evident that this statement is not in reference to Jesus returning for believers in the first resurrection or the rapture. Additionally, the statement "where I am there you may be also," was not about heaven. In John 14:10, Jesus said, I am in the Father and the Father in me." Therefore, through His death, He was providing an opportunity for us to have the same dwelling experience. How was this dwelling going to be accomplished? When Jesus said I will come again and receive you into Myself, He was referring to the coming of the Holy Spirit. Note that right after speaking about dwelling in the Father and the Father dwelling in us in the first portion of John Chapter 14 (John 14:1-14), Jesus continues the discussion. In the second portion of the chapter (John 14:15-31), He talks about the Comforter or the Holy Ghost abiding or dwelling with us. The classic mistake that is often made when reading this chapter is that the connection is not made between us dwelling in the Father and the Holy Ghost dwelling in us. Let us revisit the passage.

> 16. And I will pray the Father, and he shall give you another Comforter, that he may abide with you for ever;
>
> 17. Even the Spirit of truth; whom the world cannot receive, because it seeth him not, neither knoweth him: but ye know him; for he dwelleth with you, and shall be in you.
>
> 18. I will not leave you comfortless: I will come to you.
>
> 19. Yet a little while, and the world seeth me no more; but ye see me: because I live, ye shall live also.

20. At that day ye shall know that I am in my Father, and ye in me, and I in you.

21. He that hath my commandments, and keepeth them, he it is that loveth me: and he that loveth me shall be loved of my Father, and I will love him, and will manifest myself to him.

22. Judas saith unto him, not Iscariot, Lord, how is it that thou wilt manifest thyself unto us, and not unto the world?

23. Jesus answered and said unto him, If a man love me, he will keep my words: and my Father will love him, and we will come unto him, and make our abode with him. (John 14:16-23)

When Jesus said, "I will not leave you comfortless, I will come unto you" (in the person of the Holy Ghost), this was in fulfillment of what He said in John 14:3, "I will come again and receive you unto myself; that where I am (in the Father), there ye may be also." By the Holy Spirit dwelling in us, we simultaneously also dwell in the Father—He is in us, and we are in Him. This speaks of unity dwelling. The Holy Spirit is the Spirit of adoption (Romans 8:15); therefore, when He dwells in us, we are consequently adopted into the Father's house or His family.

In John 14:19, Jesus speaks of His death and resurrection. He says, "Because I live, you shall live also." He goes on to say in verse 20, when you receive this life (the Holy Spirit) that I shall give you then you will come into the realization that I am in the Father, ye in Me, and I in you. In other words, when you receive the Holy Ghost, you will be incorporated into the Father, and you will be where I am also. This creates the perfect illustration of unity dwelling. John 14:23 reinforces this when it says that if we love Jesus and keep His words, the Father and Son will love us and come and make their abode or dwelling in us. As we have concluded, it is the same concept of mansions expressed in John 14:2.

In summary, throughout the entire chapter, Jesus was saying that, in your current state, you are not members of the Father's house or sons. Consequently, you cannot dwell in the Father and the Father cannot dwell in you. However, because I am the way, the truth, and the life, you can have access to the Father but only through me. Through the Holy Spirit, the Father can dwell in you and you in the Father.

In reference to the questions presented at the beginning of the chapter, so far, five of the six questions have been answered. Based on the proper context of John Chapter 14, regarding the Father's house, mansions, and Jesus going to prepare a place for us, we are in a better position to answer the last question.

## 6. Where Will Believers Spend Eternity?

Now that we have a proper perspective of John Chapter 14, we are in a better position to answer the question of where believers will spend eternity. However, to understand this point, there needs to be an appreciation for God's original intent for humanity concerning the earth. This original purpose creates a proper perspective of the eternal dwelling place of believers. As a premise for understanding the Scriptures, it should be noted that the seed for all Scripture is located in the book of Genesis. Therefore, based on the account that it offers, God's original intent was for humanity to dwell on Earth and have dominion over creation (Genesis 1:26-28). Furthermore, when God created humanity, He did so in the capacity of a son (Luke 3:38). To be clear, "son" is not gender-specific but is used in Scripture based on what a son represents to the Father. Therefore, His purpose was to have government control or dominion entrusted to His sons. Hence, not only was there a kingdom environment on Earth but also a family environment. In essence, God gave His son a territory or sphere of influence or control; Adam was given the realm of Earth to exercise dominion over. This was a manifestation of the theocratic (God-rule) kingdom of God on Earth. These principles set the parameters for the discussion of God's purpose for His sons and the earth.

To truly understand the Bible, it is imperative to grasp the concept of a kingdom. In a condensed format, the Bible is simply an account of a King establishing His kingdom. As it relates to the establishment of God's kingdom, His purpose is to colonize Earth with the kingdom of heaven. However, for some reason, our governors and tutors have created a mindset that has caused us to want to go to heaven, whereas God is more interested in bringing heaven to Earth.

When God created humanity, this represented an extension of His kingdom here on Earth. In principle, God set up a colony on Earth and the intention was to colonize Earth with the culture and values of the kingdom of heaven. Colonization is the expansion of a kingdom to a foreign territory. A colony is a group of emigrants who settle in a distant territory but remain subject to or closely associated with the parent country. Therefore, Adam and Eve, though on Earth, were actually representatives of another kingdom.

However, after man's disobedience in Genesis Chapter 3, the manifestation of God's kingdom on Earth ended or, better yet, it was interrupted. Additionally, humanity became separated from both the kingdom of God and the family or house of God. Therefore, when Jesus came and announced that the kingdom of heaven was at hand, the Lord was once again bringing the governing influence or dominion of the kingdom of heaven to Earth. He was extending heaven's territory to Earth and colonizing Earth with the principles of heaven, which was His original intent. Furthermore, as we have discussed, Jesus was also charged with bringing humanity back into the Father's house or family. Hence, He said in my Father's house or family are many places for you to dwell.

Again, I reiterate that it was never the Lord's design to colonize heaven with Earth but to colonize Earth with the influence of heaven. Unfortunately, the church has been teaching the opposite of what God intends, as we will not be dwelling in heaven for all eternity. Despite the elaborate and colorful sermons that have been taught, Jesus did not leave Earth to commence a building project of "so-called" mansions in heaven for the arrival of believers (even though He was a carpenter). Though this seems to be a popular position, this notion is not supported by Scripture. Furthermore, what is the purpose of mansions in heaven if we are going to be on Earth? As we have established, the spirits of believers who have died are presently in heaven. Moreover, after the first resurrection, they will return to heaven with the Lord. However, this will not be their eternal dwelling place as they will be there for a short while.

On that note, the Bible never says that heaven is the reward for believers. In fact, Matthew 5:5 says, "Blessed are the meek: for they shall inherit the Earth." Furthermore, John 3:16 says that the gift of God is eternal life. Because the Spirit of God dwells in those that believe in Jesus, we presently have the gift of eternal life, for whoever believes in the Son of God already has eternal life (John 3:36; John 6:47).

> Verily, verily, I say unto you, He that heareth my word, and believeth in Him that sent me, hath everlasting life, and shall not come into condemnation; but is passed from death into life. (John 5:24)

Eternal life does not start when we die; it starts the moment we accept Jesus as Savior; therefore, it can be experienced now. In this regard, eternal life does not only mean unending years but also points to the quality of life. This is part of the reason Romans 5:17 says that we reign in life through Jesus Christ. Hence, eternal life pertains to quantity as well as quality.

Regarding God's kingdom on Earth, even when Jesus taught His disciples how to pray, He said, "Thy kingdom come, thy will be done in Earth, as it is in heaven" (Matthew 6:9-15). God's eternal purpose is to bring the culture of heaven to Earth. It is to bring His governing influence and His dominion to Earth through Jesus Christ and transform us into the image of His Son.

Believers today are representatives of the kingdom of God. Wherever we go, the kingdom of God is there because it is within us (Luke 17:20-21). Therefore, just like Jesus, our message is "Repent: for the kingdom of heaven is at hand." The kingdom of heaven is always at hand when the representatives of God are present. However, the second phase of the kingdom of God is the futuristic and literal kingdom that will come to Earth. The inhabitants will be those who have the kingdom of God within them or the sons of God. This kingdom is known as the messianic kingdom initiated during the millennial reign of Christ.

1. And I saw an angel come down from heaven, having the key of the bottomless pit and a great chain in his hand.

2. And he laid hold on the dragon, that old serpent, which is the Devil, and Satan, and bound him a thousand years,

3. And cast him into the bottomless pit, and shut him up, and set a seal upon him, that he should deceive the nations no more, till the thousand years should be fulfilled: and after that he must be loosed a little season.

4. And I saw thrones, and they sat upon them, and judgment was given unto them: and I saw the souls of them that were beheaded for the witness of Jesus, and for the word of God, and which had not worshipped the beast, neither his image, neither had received his mark upon their foreheads, or in their hands; and they lived and reigned with Christ a thousand years.

5. But the rest of the dead lived not again until the thousand years were finished. This is the first resurrection.

6. Blessed and holy is he that hath part in the first resurrection: on such the second death hath no power, but they shall be priests of God and of Christ, and shall reign with him a thousand years (Revelation 20:1-6).

When Christ returns to the earth (Zechariah 14:3-4), all believers who will be in heaven will return with Him. They will reign (have dominion) with Him on the earth for one thousand years. He will set up His kingdom/government on Earth with His sons. Recall from the book of Genesis that this was the Father's intent from the beginning. After the thousand years are fulfilled, the judgment of those involved in the second resurrection will occur. This is followed by a new heaven, a new earth, and the New Jerusalem coming down to Earth from heaven with God dwelling with His people on Earth for eternity.

1. And I saw a new heaven and a new earth: for the first heaven and the first earth were passed away; and there was no more sea.

2. And I John saw the holy city, new Jerusalem, coming down from God out of heaven, prepared as a bride adorned for her husband.

3. And I heard a great voice out of heaven saying, Behold, the tabernacle of God is with men, and he will dwell with them, and they shall be his people, and God himself shall be with them, and be their God.

4. And God shall wipe away all tears from their eyes; and there shall be no more death, neither sorrow, nor crying, neither shall there be any more pain: for the former things are passed away (Revelation 21:1-4).

As this chapter has detailed, there is no indication that believers will spend eternity in heaven but rather, on Earth. Even the Lord of heaven, will come to Earth and tabernacle or dwell among His people. As mentioned previously, the meek shall inherit the earth (Matthew 5:5). Therefore, the earth is considered a part of the inheritance of the people of God. Furthermore, when God made the promise to Abraham in Genesis 17:8, He indicated that the land was given to his seed as an everlasting or eternal possession. Hence, from the beginning, God's intent was for humanity to inhabit the earth and that has not changed.

The details in this chapter represent a condensed format of my book entitled, *Are There Really Mansions in Heaven? It's a Family Affair*. For a more comprehensive understanding of the content of this chapter, please refer to the book.

## Chapter Five

# HEAVEN AND HELL

No discussion on what happens when you die is complete without a comprehensive conversation on heaven and hell. Therefore, this chapter is dedicated to that exchange.

From countless anecdotes, the opinions of heaven and hell are seemingly endless. Even Hollywood by way of several movies has made contributions depicting the conditions that are believed to exist in each of these domains. They are offered as the two ultimate and eternal destinations for all of humanity; thus, there is a fascination with the perspectives presented by each one.

Based on descriptions, these two realms are seen as polar opposites of each other. Heaven is portrayed as a place of eternal life, peace, and overall bliss, whereas hell is described as a place of eternal damnation, misery, and anguish. Once again, as students of the Word of God, we must adopt the principle offered in 2 Peter 1:16, which says that the "more sure" word of prophecy or the Word of God will always take precedence over personal stories or even eyewitness accounts. Therefore, to obtain a true perspective of heaven and hell, we have to examine what the Scripture has to say rather than rely on stories, visions, or accounts of near-death experiences. Let us start the discussion with what the Bible has to say about heaven.

## HEAVEN

From previous chapters, we have already determined what happens immediately after death. Recall, that the body goes back to the dust of the earth and the spirit goes back to God. Additionally, the concept of mansions in heaven has also been disproven. Based on the proper context of Scripture, the notion of mansions refers to believers dwelling in the Father and the Father dwelling in us. It also speaks of sons being one with the Father as members of His house or family. Furthermore, salient evidence has been submitted, resulting in the conclusion that the kingdom of God will, in effect, be established on Earth where believers will spend eternity reigning with the Lord. Based on these points, the perspective of heaven offered by Scripture differs from the popular notions offered by the media and purported eyewitness accounts.

What does the Bible say about heaven? First, the Bible does not describe heaven as one general place but rather three separate realms. Such a statement may generate the question, "By what measure can we come to such a conclusion?"

In 2 Corinthians 12:2, Paul provides an account of being caught up to the third heaven. Hence, logic would suggest that if there is a third heaven, there is also a first and second heaven.

2. I knew a man in Christ above fourteen years ago, (whether in the body, I cannot tell; or whether out of the body, I cannot tell: God knoweth;) such an one caught up to the third heaven.

3. And I knew such a man, (whether in the body, or out of the body, I cannot tell: God knoweth)

4. How that he was caught up into paradise, and heard unspeakable words, which it is not lawful for a man to utter. (2 Corinthians 12:2-4)

Notice that even though Paul states that he was caught up to the third heaven, he provided no account of what he saw. Moreover, what he heard could not be spoken as it was unlawful for a man to utter it. However, today, professed eyewitnesses of heaven seem to have no such restraints. Furthermore, even when glimpses of heaven are recorded in Scripture (Acts 7:56 and Revelation Chapter 4), the versions are totally different from the ones offered by movies and many individuals today by means of dreams, near-death experiences, or visions.

Again, with many things in life, the answer or insight concerning a matter is often found in its genesis or beginning. Therefore, to understand the concept of heaven, it is best to examine the account of it as outlined in creation in the book of Genesis.

> In the beginning, God created the Heaven and the earth. (Genesis 1:1)

The word "heaven" in Genesis 1:1 is the Hebrew word *shamayim*. It is in the plural form, meaning heavens, parts of which are visible and part of which is invisible. The word "heavens" refers to three areas:

- The sky (atmosphere)
- The abode of the stars or the visible universe
- The abode of God

This is further emphasized in several other passages where the word "heavens" (the plural form) is used concerning creation.

> Thus the heavens and the earth were finished, and all the host of them. (Genesis 2:1)

> These are the generations of the heavens and of the earth when they were created, in the day that the Lord God made the earth and the heavens. (Genesis 2:4)

> For all the gods of the people are idols: but the Lord made the heavens. (1 Chronicles 16:26)
>
> By the word of the Lord were the heavens made; and all the hosts of them by the breath of His mouth. (Psalm 33:6)
>
> Of old hast thou laid the foundation of the earth: and the heavens are the work of thy hands. (Psalm 102:25)
>
> Thus saith God the Lord, He that created the heavens and stretched them out. (Isaiah 42:5)

To explain the fullness of heaven, all that it incorporates, or all its dimensions, the Bible uses the term "heaven and heaven of heavens" (1 Kings 8:27, 2 Chronicles 2:6, 2 Chronicles 6:18). Therefore, based on the plural usage of the word "heavens" in Scripture, Paul's account of being caught up to the third heaven and the definition of heavens, let us examine the three distinct levels or heights of heaven.

## THE FIRST HEAVEN

The first heaven consists of Earth's atmosphere, which is also referred to as the firmament or the sky (Genesis 1:6-8). It is the expanse in which the birds and planes fly, where the clouds are, and where the rain and other weather-related occurrences come from. It is the atmosphere surrounding Earth. Even though the sky does not actually end (hence the phrase, the sky is the limit) a common dividing line where space officially starts is about 67 miles up. Some passages of Scripture that speak to the first heaven are listed below:

> And out of the ground the Lord God formed every beast of the field, and every fowl of <u>the air.</u> (Genesis 2:1)

The word "air" in this passage is the same Hebrew word for heaven, which is *shamayim*.

> 11. In the sixth hundredth year of Noah's life, in the second month, the seventeenth day of the month, the same day were the fountains of the deep broken up, and <u>the windows (floodgates) of heaven were opened.</u>
>
> 12. And the rain was upon the earth forty days and forty nights. (Genesis 7:11-12)

> Therefore God give thee of the <u>dew of heaven</u> and the fatness of the earth, and plenty of corn and wine. (Genesis 27:28)

> And then the Lord's wrath be kindled against you, and He <u>shut up the heaven, that there be no rain</u>, and that the land yield not her fruit; and lest ye perish quickly from off the good land which the Lord giveth you. (Deuteronomy 11:17)

> And it came to pass in the meanwhile, that the <u>heaven was black with clouds and wind, and there was great rain.</u> (1 Kings 18:45)

> For as <u>the rain cometh down</u>, and <u>the snow from heaven</u>, and returneth not thither, but watereth the earth, and maketh it bring forth and bud, that it may give seed to the sower, and bread to the eater. (Isaiah 55:10)

> Nevertheless, He left not Himself without witness, in that He did good, and gave us <u>rain from heaven</u>, and fruitful seasons filling our hearts with food and gladness. (Acts 14:17)

## THE SECOND HEAVEN

The second heaven, which Scripture also refers to as the firmament (expanse), consists of outer space. This comprises of celestial bodies such as the sun, moon, and stars. Some of the scriptures that speak to this are listed below:

> 14. And God said, Let there be <u>lights in the firmament of the heaven</u> to divide the day from the night; and let them be for signs, and for seasons, and for days, and years:
>
> 15. And let them be for <u>lights in the firmament of the heaven to give</u> light upon the earth: and it was so.
>
> <u>16. And God made two great lights; the greater light to rule the day, and the lesser light to rule the night: he made the stars also.</u>
>
> <u>17. And God set them in the firmament of the heaven to give light upon the earth,</u>
>
> 18. And to rule over the day and over the night, and to divide the light from the darkness: and God saw that it was good. (Genesis 1:14-18)

> And I will make thy seed to multiply as <u>the stars of heaven</u>, and will give unto thy seed all these countries; and in thy seed shall all the nations of the earth be blessed. (Genesis 26:4)

> Remember Abraham, Isaac, and Israel, thy servants, to whom thou swarest by thine own self, and saidst unto them, I will multiply your seed as <u>the stars of heaven</u>, and all this land that I have spoken of will I give unto your seed, and they shall inherit it forever. (Exodus 32:13)

> For the <u>stars of heaven and the constellations</u> thereof shall not give their light: the sun shall be darkened in

his going forth, and the moon shall not cause her light to shine. (Isaiah 13:10)

And they shall spread them before <u>the sun, and the moon, and all the host of heaven</u>, whom they have loved, and whom they have served, and after whom they have walked, and whom they have sought, and whom they have worshipped: they shall not be gathered, nor be buried; they shall be for dung upon the face of the earth. (Jeremiah 8:2)

Immediately after the tribulation of those days shall <u>the sun be darkened, and the moon shall not give her light, and the stars shall fall from heaven, and the powers of the heavens shall be shaken.</u> (Matthew 24:29)

## THE THIRD HEAVEN

The third heaven refers to the dwelling place of God where His throne is. It is the highest heaven. This is the place where Paul was caught up to, where Ezekiel had visions of God, and what was opened to John while on the Isle of Patmos.

> The LORD is in his holy temple, <u>the LORD'S throne is in heaven</u>: his eyes behold, his eyelids try, the children of men. (Psalm 11:4)

> Now it came to pass in the thirtieth year, in the fourth month, in the fifth day of the month, as I was among the captives by the river of Chebar, that <u>the heavens were opened, and I saw visions of God.</u> (Ezekiel 1:1)

> And said, Behold, <u>I see the heavens opened, and the Son of man standing on the right hand of God.</u> (Acts 7:56)

1. It is not expedient for me doubtless to glory. I will come to visions and revelations of the Lord.

2. I knew a man in Christ above fourteen years ago, (whether in the body, I cannot tell; or whether out of the body, I cannot tell: God knoweth;) such an one <u>caught up to the third heaven.</u>

3. And I knew such a man, (whether in the body, or out of the body, I cannot tell: God knoweth)

4. How that he was <u>caught up into paradise</u>, and heard unspeakable words, which it is not lawful for a man to utter. (2 Corinthians 12:1-4)

14. Seeing then that we have a great high priest, that is <u>passed into the heavens, Jesus the Son of God</u>, let us hold fast our profession.

15. For we have not an high priest which cannot be touched with the feeling of our infirmities; but was in all points tempted like as we are, yet without sin.

6. Let us therefore come boldly unto the throne of grace, that we may obtain mercy, and find grace to help in time of need. (Hebrews 4:14-16)

1. After this I looked, and, behold, <u>a door was opened in heaven</u>: and the first voice which<u> I heard was as</u> it were of a trumpet talking with me; which said, Come up hither, and I will shew thee things which must be hereafter.

2. And immediately I was in the spirit: and, behold, <u>a throne was set in heaven, and one sat on the throne.</u> (Revelation 4:1-2)

Now that we have a good understanding of heaven in all of its facets (as Scripture allows us to know), we can examine what the Word of God has to say concerning hell.

## HELL

In the Old Testament, the word used for hell is the Hebrew word *sheol*, which means the following:

- The grave
- The pit
- The abode of the dead
- The place of departed spirits
- A place of extreme degradation in sin (figuratively)
- A place of exile (figuratively)

In many references in the Old Testament, *sheol* or hell <u>does not</u> refer to a place of eternal fire or punishment. It refers to the place of the dead, which includes the abode of both the righteous and the wicked. In other references, it figuratively points to the condition of the dead or a state of deprivation. Predominately, *sheol* or hell <u>was not</u> thought of as a place of eternal punishment but simply the place of departed spirits. Several scriptures that support the definitions are listed below:

> And all his sons and all his daughters rose up to comfort him; but he refused to be comforted; and he said, <u>For I will go down into the grave unto my son mourning</u>. Thus his father wept for him. (Genesis 37:35)

> They shall go down to <u>the bars of the pit</u>, when our rest together is in the dust. (Job 17:16)

> For thou wilt not leave my <u>soul in hell</u>; neither wilt thou suffer thine Holy One to see corruption. (Psalm 16:10)

This is in reference to Jesus Christ and the term "soul in hell" refers to Him not being left in *sheol* meaning the place of departed spirits. Also, he did not see corruption meaning while in the grave, His body did not decompose.

> O LORD, thou hast brought up my soul from the grave: thou hast kept me alive, that I should not go down to the pit. (Psalm 30:3)

> If I ascend up into heaven, thou art there: if I make my bed in hell, behold, thou art there. (Psalm 139:8)

> Thou shalt beat him with the rod, and shalt deliver his soul from hell. (Proverbs 23:14)

In the New Testament, three words are used for hell: *hades*, *tartaroo* and *geenna or gehenna*. Let us examine the three in detail.

## HADES

In Greek mythology, Hades was the god of the lower region or underworld and ruler of the dead. This concept, fueled by movies such as "Clash of the Titans," has created the perception that *hades* or hell, when mentioned in Scripture, also represents the underworld with similar conditions. However, *hades* or hell in the New Testament is the Hebrew equivalent to *sheol* in the Old Testament. It similarly refers to the grave or the abode of the dead. It does not subscribe to the notion of eternal fire. Additionally, as also outlined in the Old Testament, it refers to the dead or the place or state of the dead. Notice that in the New Testament, death is normally associated with hell (grave) as they are related.

> And thou, Capernaum, which art exalted unto heaven, shalt be brought down to hell: for if the mighty works,

which have been done in thee, had been done in Sodom, it would have remained until this day. (Matthew 11:23)

And I say also unto thee, That thou art Peter, and upon this rock I will build my church; and the gates of hell shall not prevail against it (Gates are symbolic of stronghold or power). (Matthew 16:18)

Because thou wilt not leave my soul in hell, neither wilt thou suffer thine Holy One to see corruption. (Acts 2:27)

He seeing this before spake of the resurrection of Christ, that his soul was not left in hell, neither his flesh did see corruption. (Acts 2:31)

O death, where is thy sting? O grave, where is thy victory? (1 Corinthians 15:55)

And cast him into the bottomless pit, and shut him up, and set a seal upon him, that he should deceive the nations no more, till the thousand years should be fulfilled: and after that he must be loosed a little season. (Revelation 20:13)

# TARTAROO

The second Greek word for hell in the New Testament is the word *tartaroo*, which is the name of the subterranean region, a dark place of wretchedness and sorrow. It was regarded by the ancient Greeks as the abode of the wicked dead, where they suffer punishment for their evil deeds. 2 Peter 2:4 refers to it as the place where the angels who sinned are being held in chains until judgment. It corresponds to the Jewish recognition of *gehenna,* which is the third Greek word used to illustrate hell in the New Testament.

> For if God spared not the angels that sinned, but cast them down to hell, and delivered them into chains of darkness, to be reserved unto judgment. (2 Peter 2:4)

## GEHENNA

The third Greek word used to describe hell in the New Testament is *gehenna*, which is derived from the valley of the son of Hinnom, located south of Jerusalem (Joshua 15:8). It was the place where children were sacrificed to the Ammonite god Moloch (2 Kings 23:10). Later in Jeremiah 7:30-33, the valley was cursed and declared to be a burial place for criminals, a place of judgement, and a slaughter place for animals where their bodies were burned. Eventually, it also became a place for burning garbage. In the New Testament, the valley was figuratively referred to as hell being the final destination of the wicked. Therefore, when referring to eternal judgment and punishment, Jesus used the reference of the burning valley, *gehenna*, that the Jews were quite familiar with. Unlike *hades*, all the references for *gehenna* in the New Testament except for James 3:6 are associated with eternal fire, judgement, and punishment, which are linked to the lake of fire in Revelation 21:8.

> But I say unto you, That whosoever is angry with his brother without a cause shall be in danger of the judgment: and whosoever shall say to his brother, Raca, shall be in danger of the council: but whosoever shall say, Thou fool, shall be in danger of hell fire. (Matthew 5:22)

> 43. And if thy hand offend thee, cut it off: it is better for thee to enter into life maimed, than having two hands to go into hell, into the fire that never shall be quenched:
>
> 44. Where their worm dieth not, and the fire is not quenched.

45. And if thy foot offend thee, cut it off: it is better for thee to enter halt into life, than having two feet to be cast into hell, into the fire that never shall be quenched:

46. Where their worm dieth not, and the fire is not quenched.

47. And if thine eye offend thee, pluck it out: it is better for thee to enter into the kingdom of God with one eye, than having two eyes to be cast into hell fire:

48. Where their worm dieth not, and the fire is not quenched. (Mark 9:43-48)

> And the tongue is a fire, a world of iniquity: so is the tongue among our members, that it defileth the whole body, and setteth on fire the course of nature; and it is set on fire of hell. (James 3:6)

So, there you have it, a scriptural digest of heaven and hell. Certainly, by now, there should be a better appreciation of the two domains and an elimination of all the speculation brought about by untamed imaginations. Unlike the example provided in 2 Peter 1:16, most of the stories we hear and movies we see are based on cunningly devised fables, which do not mirror the truth of Scripture. The concept of hell and all its dimensions (based on what the Scripture details) will be further discussed in the next chapter.

## Chapter Six

# ABRAHAM'S BOSOM

## THE RICH MAN AND LAZARUS

Now that we have a better understanding of the variations of heaven and hell, we are positioned for a better perspective regarding their specific mention in the New Testament. In that vein, let us begin with an examination of Jesus' account of the rich man and Lazarus.

19. There was a certain rich man, which was clothed in purple and fine linen, and fared sumptuously every day:

20. And there was a certain beggar named Lazarus, which was laid at his gate, full of sores,

21. And desiring to be fed with the crumbs which fell from the rich man's table: moreover the dogs came and licked his sores.

22. And it came to pass, that the beggar died, and was carried by the angels into Abraham's bosom: the rich man also died, and was buried;

23. And in hell he lift up his eyes, being in torments, and seeth Abraham afar off, and Lazarus in his bosom.

24. And he cried and said, Father Abraham, have mercy on me, and send Lazarus, that he may dip the tip of his finger in water, and cool my tongue; for I am tormented in this flame.

25. But Abraham said, Son, remember that thou in thy lifetime receivedst thy good things, and likewise Lazarus evil things: but now he is comforted, and thou art tormented.

26. And beside all this, between us and you there is a great gulf fixed: so that they which would pass from hence to you cannot; neither can they pass to us, that would come from thence.

27. Then he said, I pray thee therefore, father, that thou wouldest send him to my father's house:

28. For I have five brethren; that he may testify unto them, lest they also come into this place of torment.

29. Abraham saith unto him, They have Moses and the prophets; let them hear them.

30. And he said, Nay, father Abraham: but if one went unto them from the dead, they will repent.

31. And he said unto him, If they hear not Moses and the prophets, neither will they be persuaded, though one rose from the dead. (Luke 16:19-31)

It is often debated that the narrative of the rich man and Lazarus was not a real story but a parable similar to that of the lost (prodigal) son or the others Jesus told to explain a spiritual principle. Those who take this position argue that even though the beggar had a name, this does not certify that the event actually took place. This is despite the fact that Jesus did not provide a name for any character in the other parables He told. In this regard, their argument is based on the premise that the name "Lazarus," in Hebrew points to a man who is destitute of help or one "whom God helps." Therefore, they submit that the name was simply a fitting character for the story. Nevertheless, regardless of the perspective held, it is the substance of the account that is most important. Oftentimes, we get so caught up in the minor details that we miss the principle being expressed. In all the parables that Jesus told, there was always a relevant truth that He was conveying. Additionally, when we examine the story using the whole of Scripture context, we will discover that the principles of the account are in harmony with other scriptures. Therefore, I submit that not only is the story based on an actual event but at the end of this chapter it will be validated by Scripture.

The purpose of the account was to provide a vivid illustration in support of the message Jesus conveyed earlier in the chapter. In Luke 16:13, Jesus said: "No servant can serve two masters: for either he will hate the one, and love the other; or else he will hold to the one, and despise the other. Ye cannot serve God and mammon." He was addressing the covetous behavior of the Pharisees; therefore, the story serves as a visual example of what He had said previously.

Additionally, the narrative was not intended to simply contrast the wealthy with the poor; there is a more profound principle involved. Being wealthy in itself is not the grounds for condemnation. However, the rich man by being a servant of the riches he possessed drew disapproval from Jesus. Based on the context of the entire passage, this was the primary message Jesus was communicating. Furthermore, the story highlights that the rich man had no compassion for the poor. In fact, Lazarus received more sympathy from the dogs who licked his sores than he did from the rich man. Therefore, judgment was centered more on the rich man's actions and the condition of his heart than the mere fact that he was rich. Additionally, it is also safe to conclude that being poor does not necessitate righteous standing either.

Now that the marginal details have been addressed, let us look at the particulars of the account. The story creates a contrast between a certain rich man and a beggar whose name was Lazarus. Despite the inequality surrounding the circumstances of their lives on Earth, the Scripture provides an equalizer and says they both died. Regardless of great wealth or the absence of it, the appointment with death is inevitable. Recall that Ecclesiastes 9:2-3 says that is the event that happens to us all. The account says that Lazarus died and was carried by angels to Abraham's bosom, and the rich man went to hell. Even though the account does not provide the precise conditions that existed in Abraham's bosom, the contrasting conditions of hell produce a comparative perspective. However, as we will discover later in this chapter, the conditions of Abraham's bosom resemble the environment of the garden of Eden.

The word "bosom" in the passage is the Greek word *kolpos*. It speaks of one who reclines at the table so that his head rests on the bosom or breast of the one next to him. An example of this is provided in John 21:20. It is a place of honor, reserved for special guests, and means to be at someone's side. Therefore, the term "Abraham's bosom" means to obtain a seat next to Abraham or to be a partaker with him—the host. Abraham is associated with the promise God made to him, as well as righteousness. Therefore, it was a figurative reference to the place where the righteous dead who were partakers with Abraham went. We will delve more into the usage of the term "Abraham's bosom" in the next section.

As mentioned in the previous chapter, the Hebrew word used to indicate the place of departed spirits or the realm of the dead is *sheol*. The Greek equivalent for *sheol* is the word *hades;* they are both translated as hell. Based on the illustration in the account of the rich man and Lazarus, the place of departed spirits or the realm of the dead had two distinct compartments, which were separated by an impassable gulf. One section was designated for the righteous and the other for the unrighteous. By contrasting Abraham's bosom with the conditions of the torment section of hell, Abraham's bosom was seen as a place of rest, peace, and contentment.

As opposed to Abraham's bosom, when the rich man died, it says that he went to hell or specifically, the portion of hell reserved for the unrighteous. Notice that despite being dead, the rich man was conscious, had feelings, was concerned about his family, and was able to conduct a rational conversation. Of note, this does not contradict Ecclesiastes 12:9, which says that the dead know nothing. As mentioned previously, this verse distinctly refers to knowledge or consciousness of what is happening "under the sun" or on the earth.

The parable describes hell as a place of torments even though it does not say specifically what all of them are. However, based on the rich man's experience, he refers to the flames, which obviously contribute to the torments. In fact, the anguish was so great, his plea was for Lazarus to come, dip his finger in water, and touch his tongue in order to provide some relief.

Furthermore, the rich man in his conversation with Abraham makes another petition. He requests that Lazarus be sent back to his brothers to inform them of the torment of hell so they may avoid it. However, Abraham's response was, "They have Moses and the prophets; let them hear them." In other words, they have the Scriptures, or the written Word of God, which represents a "more sure" word of prophecy (2 Peter 1:16-21). Nevertheless, the rich man was convinced that someone from the dead would offer a more compelling argument in helping his brothers repent. However, Abraham offers a resounding and thought-provoking response to that suggestion. He says that if they don't give heed to the Scriptures, neither will they be persuaded if one rose from the dead and rehearsed the account regarding the conditions of hell.

Abraham, therefore, was putting more stock in the written Word of God than someone's personal account. Hence, despite the many descriptive illustrations that abound citing the conditions of hell, the persuasive power of the Word of God remains the best resource in turning humanity to righteousness.

It should be noted that both Abraham's bosom and hell presented in this account were temporary holding areas. They are not the eternal destination of the righteous or the wicked. As it pertains to the righteous, we will discuss that later in this chapter. Furthermore, despite the torment currently being experienced by those in hell, Revelation 20:14 says that death and hell will be cast into the lake of fire. This speaks of *gehenna* mentioned in the previous chapter and constitutes the second death.

## Abraham's Bosom

In the account of the rich man and Lazarus, Jesus uses the term "Abraham's bosom" to figuratively identify the place where Lazarus went when he died. Based on the reconciliation of Scripture, it is agreed that paradise is synonymous with Abraham's bosom as they are the same place. In fact, this was the temporary location where all the righteous men and women went prior to Jesus' resurrection. Why is paradise referred to as Abraham's bosom? On that note, why did He specifically call it "Abraham's bosom?" Why didn't He just say paradise as He did to the thief on the cross?

First, it had to do with the audience and the message He wanted to convey. Recall that in Luke Chapter 16, Jesus was speaking to the Pharisees who regarded Abraham as their father (John 8:39), and they held him in high esteem. In Genesis 12:1-3, God made a promise to Abraham that in him all nations shall be blessed. Furthermore, to guarantee the promise and to make it immutable (unchangeable and eternal), Hebrews 6:13-18 says that God swore by Himself. Therefore, the promise to Abraham was an unconditional covenant and those associated with Abraham are beneficiaries of the same promise. Also, from the previous discussion, the word "bosom" signifies being a partaker with someone. Therefore, Abraham's bosom is figuratively ascribed to those who died in righteousness and would eventually be partakers of his promise. Hence, the term directly connects Lazarus to the promise that God gave to Abraham. To be affiliated with Abraham was a matter of privilege and blessing. For that reason, based on who He was addressing, and more importantly, what Abraham represented, the association with Abraham was deliberate as it connected Lazarus to the blessings of the promise.

Furthermore, to have an appreciation for this entire context, there has to be an understanding of what the promise is. Without question, God's promise to Abraham is a matter of great significance, not only for Israel but as a cornerstone for the new covenant and every believer. This is evident as throughout the New Testament it is often referred to as "the promise," "the promises" or "the blessing of Abraham" (Romans 4:13, Romans 9:4, Hebrews 11:39). In fact, in packaging what was said, Galatians 3:8 says that when God made the promise to Abraham, He was actually preaching the gospel message to him. Therefore, contained within the promise is the entirety of the gospel of Christ.

On that point, Galatians 3:16 says that God not only made the promise to Abraham but also to His seed, Jesus Christ. Therefore, Christ was the one destined to fulfill the promise. What exactly is the promise? In very plain language, Acts 3:25-26 says precisely what the promise is:

> 25. Ye are the children of the prophets, and of the covenant which God made with our fathers, saying unto Abraham, And in thy seed shall all the kindreds of the earth be blessed.
>
> *26. Unto you first God, having raised up his Son Jesus, sent him to bless you, in turning away every one of you from his iniquities.*

Therefore, the promise that God made to Abraham involved redemption through Jesus Christ. The word "redemption" speaks of being released based on the payment of a ransom. When Adam sinned, sin exercised dominion or authority over humanity and held us captive. However, through Jesus' sacrifice, that control ended as the price was paid (Romans 6:9). Furthermore, the term "turning away" means to no longer be in allegiance to something, which supports the fact that the dominion of sin has ended for those who accept Jesus (Romans 6:14). Hence, the promise to Abraham was more than just the forgiveness of sins; it involved changing our inner man or spirit from the very nature of sin. It is a promise of righteousness. It speaks of rebirth or being born of the Spirit, which makes us new creatures (2 Corinthians 5:17).

Galatians 3:14 provides more perspective on the subject by adding, "That the blessing of Abraham might come on the Gentiles through Jesus Christ; that we might receive the promise of the Spirit through faith." *Therefore, in its fullness, the promise that God made to Abraham is the Holy Spirit dwelling in humanity, thereby making us new creatures resulting in eternal redemption and eternal inheritance* (Hebrews 9:11-15). The righteous who died prior to Christ did not experience this transformation or the benefits of the promise; therefore, they went to a holding place until the promise was fulfilled.

In summary, Jesus referred to paradise as Abraham's bosom considering the promise that was made to Abraham. Those who died and were imputed righteousness, upon death went to paradise or figuratively, Abraham's bosom until the fulfillment of the promise. Therefore, once Christ fulfilled the promise they were partakers of eternal redemption and eternal inheritance. This is what Hebrews 11:39-40 is referring to when it says that even though the righteous mentioned throughout the chapter obtained a good report through faith, they did not receive "the promise." This was because the fulfillment of Abraham's promise represented the "better thing" that would make them perfect or complete in terms of redemption. This point will be discussed in greater detail in short order. However, there first has to be a reconciliation of Jesus' conversation with the thief on the cross.

## TODAY YOU SHALL BE WITH ME IN PARADISE

> 39. And one of the malefactors which were hanged railed on him, saying, If thou be Christ, save thyself and us.
>
> 40. But the other answering rebuked him, saying, Dost not thou fear God, seeing thou art in the same condemnation?
>
> 41. And we indeed justly; for we receive the due reward of our deeds: but this man hath done nothing amiss.
>
> 42. And he said unto Jesus, Lord, remember me when thou comest into thy kingdom.
>
> 43. And Jesus said unto him, Verily I say unto thee, To day shalt thou be with me in paradise. (Luke 23:39-43)

There has been much debate concerning the context of the statement, which Jesus made to the thief while He was on the cross. In responding to the thief regarding remembering him when He comes into His kingdom, Jesus answers and said, "I say to you today thou shalt be with me in paradise." Part of the debate regarding this verse pertains to the proper placement of the comma, which drastically changes the context of the statement. The position of the comma makes a significant difference in the meaning and understanding of a sentence as it instructs the reader when to pause and has an impact on emphasis.

One of the more interesting examples I found regarding the placement of the comma is outlined below. Notice how the meaning and context of the sentence are totally altered (in fact, it is the opposite) based on where the comma is positioned.

- Woman, without her man, is nothing.
- Woman, without her, man is nothing.

As the example reveals, where the comma is placed is of great significance. It should be noted that when Scripture was originally written, it did not contain commas as they did not exist. The modern comma was not introduced until the 1400s, and it was subsequently inserted in Scripture during its translation. In this regard, let us look at the statement Jesus made to the thief while considering two options regarding the placement of the comma.

- Verily I say unto you, today thou shall be with me in paradise.
- Verily I say unto you today, thou shall be with me in paradise.

Notice as with the first example, the position of the comma completely changes the context, meaning, and understanding of the statement that is being conveyed, thereby impacting what is eventually understood and believed. Is Jesus saying, "Today, you will be with me in paradise?" Or is He saying that He is making the statement today? I contend that the former reigns over the latter as he was meeting Jesus in paradise or Abraham's bosom that very day. Apart from the argument surrounding the comma, the burden of proof rests in determining where did Jesus go when He died?

First, let us rule out where Jesus *did not* go when He died.

## HEAVEN

According to Scripture, He did not ascend to heaven to the Father. In John 20:17, immediately after His resurrection, He said to Mary Magdalene, "Touch me not; for I am not yet ascended to my Father: but go to my brethren, and say unto them, I ascend unto my Father, and your Father; and to my God, and your God." Therefore, up to this point, even after His resurrection, Jesus had not yet ascended to heaven, so it is safe to rule that out. Furthermore, as mentioned in Chapter 3, the reason He could not be touched was that He had not yet fulfilled His High Priest responsibilities in the heavenly tabernacle as foreshadowed by the law (Hebrews 9:11-12). Hence, after He went to heaven and returned, He could then be touched by His disciples (Luke 24:39).

## Hell (The side of torments- where the rich man went)

Based on the wording in the Apostle's Creed, it is widely believed that when Jesus died, He descended into hell. At face value, and from a general perspective, there is some truth to this statement, but without specificity, the Creed also allows for great ambiguity. Nevertheless, the Word of God is abundantly clear regarding where He went.

As mentioned previously, in Hebrew, the word for hell is *sheol*. It refers to the place of the dead or the place of departed spirits. This corresponds to the New Testament usage of the word *hades,* which is the Greek equivalent. As it pertains to the realm of the dead or hell, Scripture identifies two separate and distinct sections where departed spirits went upon death. One portion was known as Abraham's bosom or paradise and the other side was a place of torments (Luke 16:19-31). So, while it is true that Jesus did, indeed, go to hell when He died, Scripture is clear that He specifically went to the section referred to as paradise or Abraham's bosom. This is where all the righteous dead went before the resurrection of Jesus Christ. Based on the "whole of Scripture" perspective, there is no evidence that when Jesus died, He went to the side of hell with torments as described by the rich man in the account of the rich man and Lazarus.

While on the cross, just before Jesus was about to die, He said in Luke 23:46, "Father, into thy hands I commend my spirit." This statement simply signifies the basis of death that it is the separation of the spirit from the body. This does not mean that He went to heaven as we have discovered, but simply that His spirit was committed to the Father's charge. Furthermore, David, in referring to Jesus' death and resurrection says in Psalm 16:10, "For thou wilt not leave my soul in hell; neither wilt thou suffer thine Holy One to see corruption." This verse is also echoed in Acts 2:27. First, the word "soul" in this verse is synonymous with spirit; recall that they are sometimes used interchangeably in Scripture. Therefore, after His death, Jesus went to the section of *hades* referred to as paradise or Abraham's bosom. However, after three days, He resurrected; hence, His soul/spirit was not left in hell.

Furthermore, in reference to His body, it adds that He did not see corruption. This speaks to the fact that while in the grave, Jesus' body did not see corruption or experience decomposition. Therefore, His body was in the grave, but His spirit went to hell.

It should be reiterated that hell (where the rich man went) is a temporary abode for the dead and is distinct from the lake of fire mentioned in Revelation 20:13-15. Despite the difference presented in Scripture, many people still confuse the two. As witnessed in the case of the rich man, the unrighteous are presently in the torment side of hell, but they are not yet in the lake of fire. It is a temporary realm of condemnation and judgment. Revelation 20:14 says that death and hell will be cast into the lake of fire, which represents the second death. The lake of fire, therefore, is the eternal and final place of judgment for the unrighteous.

Included in the incorrect narrative that Jesus went to the torment side of hell when He died, is the popular storyline that while He was there, He confronted the devil and snatched the keys of hell and death. I find that vivid imaginations sometimes replace the truth of the Scriptures to create a more dramatic narrative. Indeed, through His death, Jesus defeated death, but this was accomplished through His resurrection rather than confrontation with the devil.

One verse of Scripture that is used out of context to create such an illustration is Acts 2:24, which says, "Whom God hath raised up, having loosed the pains of death: because it was not possible that He should be holden of it." A misunderstanding of this passage would give the impression that Jesus was engaged in a struggle with the devil after death, but that is inaccurate. Additionally, this does not mean that

Jesus suffered anything after death but simply that the grave could not hold Him. In fact, in harmony with the context of the entire passage, Acts 2:27, which we have already discussed supports this position. As death is a confining force from which there was no escape, when Jesus resurrected, the phrase used to describe it is "having loosed the pains of death." Therefore, the statement simply speaks of His liberty over death as a result of His resurrection. In fact, the same will be said of the righteous or the dead in Christ who will be involved in the first resurrection when mortal shall put on immortality.

> 54. So when this corruptible shall have put on incorruption, and this mortal shall have put on immortality, then shall be brought to pass the saying that is written, Death is swallowed up in victory.
>
> 55. O death, where is thy sting? O grave where is thy victory?
>
> 56. The sting of death is sin; and the strength of sin is the law. (1 Corinthians 15:54-56)

Furthermore, Ephesians Chapter 4 with the statement, "He led captivity captive," also speaks to Jesus' resurrection and His triumph over death.

> 8. Wherefore he saith, When he ascended up on high, he led captivity captive, and gave gifts unto men.
>
> 9. (Now that he ascended, what is it but that he also descended first into the lower parts of the earth?
>
> 10. He that descended is the same also that ascended up far above all heavens, that he might fill all things.) (Ephesians 4:8-10)

Again, this passage has nothing to do with a post-death engagement with the devil or some ensuing battle in hell. The term "lower parts of the earth" refers to His death and the grave just as the reference "ascended up on high" speaks of His resurrection. Moreover, the phrase, "led captivity captive" is the same as "being loosed from the pains of death" mentioned in Acts 2:24. Therefore, with death being a confining or imprisoning force that holds all men captive, when He ascended on high, or when He resurrected, He overcame what overcomes all men: death. He led captive, the captor.

In many respects, Jesus' death and resurrection serve as an example of the resurrection of believers though there are meaningful differences. Nevertheless, after three days, Jesus' spirit reunited with His body, and He was resurrected with a glorified body. Similarly, when the Lord returns, our spirits will be reunited with our bodies, which were sown in the ground but will be changed from mortal to immortal, and we will also lead captivity captive.

Now that we have determined where Jesus did not go when He died, let us discuss where He did go.

## Paradise

Based on His own admission, in Luke 23:43, Jesus said to the thief on the cross, "Today shalt thou be with me in paradise." As mentioned, the word "paradise" is synonymous with Abraham's bosom, which we have already discussed. Therefore, when Jesus died, that is where He and the thief went as he was imputed righteousness while on the cross. Moreover, that is where all the righteous dead throughout the Old Testament went before Jesus' resurrection.

## The Spirits in Prison

In addition to paradise, 1 Peter 3:18-20 points out that Jesus also went and preached to the spirits in prison.

> 18. For Christ also hath once suffered for sins, the just for the unjust, that he might bring us to God, being put to death in the flesh, but quickened by the Spirit:

> 19. By which also he went and preached unto the spirits in prison;
>
> 20. Which sometime were disobedient, when once the longsuffering of God waited in the days of Noah, while the ark was a preparing, wherein few, that is, eight souls were saved by water.

Admittedly, this passage of Scripture has been the subject of many opinions and reasoning over the years. Without going into detail about the range of assumptions that exist, it is always best to allow the Bible to interpret itself. First, the passage speaks of events that transpired after Jesus' death. Therefore, not only did Jesus go to paradise but He also went and preached unto the spirits in prison. As we have determined from Scripture, the word "spirits" is used to describe the state that human beings are in after death, which is our true unclothed essence. Hence, 1 Peter 3:19, says that these "spirits" were in prison or in holding. Furthermore, the passage provides a specific timeframe in which these people lived. What is significant about this period?

As a premise, the Bible says that sin is not imputed where there is no law.

> 13. For until the law sin was in the world. but sin is not imputed when there is no law.
>
> 14. Nevertheless death reigned from Adam to Moses, even over them that had not sinned after the similitude of Adam's transgression. (Romans 5:13-14)

The word "impute" means to set to one's account or to lay to one's charge. Therefore, before the law of Moses was instituted, even though death reigned, sin could not be charged to the people who lived during this time because there were no criteria to judge people by. There was no instrument by which to measure their actions. The exception to this was murder as noted in Genesis 9:5-6. Paul provides a good example in Romans 7:7 when he says, "I had not known sin, but by the law: for I had not known lust, except the law had said, Thou shalt not covet." It was the law that brought an awareness of what covetousness was along with other things.

In fact, this principle can be applied to a broad range of circumstances. For example, if I drive at 100 mph and there is no statute regulating the speed limit, I cannot be cited for an infraction. However, if there is a law that restricts the speed limit to 70 mph, then I can be penalized for the disobedience. Similarly, from the time of Adam up to the time of Moses, (when the law was implemented) wrongdoing or sin could not be laid to anyone's charge (even though death reigned). One of the high points during this timeframe included the tremendous wickedness of the people during the time of Noah. This is evident in Genesis 6:5-6, which says,

> 5. And GOD saw that the wickedness of man was great in the earth, and that every imagination of the thoughts of his heart was only evil continually.
>
> 6. And it repented the LORD that he had made man on the earth, and it grieved him at his heart.

Despite their wickedness, due to the absence of law, when these people died, they could not be subjected to the judgment of hell and consequently eternal judgment. Hence, they were held in a prison or a "holding area." This scripture is a perfect example of the righteousness of God, for judgment is reserved specifically for those who violate the law. Therefore, when Christ died He not only went to paradise, but He also went to preach to the spirits in prison, thereby offering them exoneration.

## ABSENT FROM THE BODY, PRESENT WITH THE LORD

> 6. Therefore we are always confident, knowing that, whilst we are at home in the body, we are absent from the Lord:
>
> 7. (For we walk by faith, not by sight:)

8. We are confident, I say, and willing rather to be absent from the body, and to be present with the Lord.

9. Wherefore we labour, that, whether present or absent, we may be accepted of him.

10. For we must all appear before the judgment seat of Christ; that every one may receive the things done in his body, according to that he hath done, whether it be good or bad. (2 Corinthians 5:6-10)

One of the greatest recognitions that we can make about who we truly are is the acknowledgment that we are spirit beings. This is the essence of our lives and our physical bodies are simply temporary residences. In appreciation of this, 2 Corinthians 5:6 points out that for believers, as long as we are at home in our bodies, we are absent from the Lord. However, Paul says that he would rather be absent from the body and present with the Lord. Being at home in our bodies makes us simultaneously absent from the Lord. On the other hand, death makes us instantaneously present with the Lord. Unlike before the resurrection of Jesus Christ, there is no temporary holding place upon death for the righteous. We (our spirits) immediately go to be with the Lord in heaven. Nevertheless, the passage concludes that whether we are absent or present from the Lord, the most important thing is to be accepted by Him. This requires a life of righteousness.

Paul expresses the same sentiment regarding dying and being with Christ in Philippians 1:23-24:

23. For I am in a strait betwixt two, having a desire to depart, and to be with Christ; which is far better:

24. Nevertheless to abide in the flesh is more needful for you. (Philippians 1:23-24)

In this instance, Paul declares that he is torn between two desires. One serves his own benefit, while the alternative benefits others. One is to depart and be with Christ, which is not just better but far better, while the other is to stay in the flesh or in his temporary home so that he may be of service to the body of Christ. Nevertheless, understanding the need of the church, he concludes that remaining was the better choice.

How is it that since Christ's resurrection, upon death, believers in Christ go immediately to be with the Lord in heaven, whereas before Christ's resurrection, the righteous went to Abraham's bosom or paradise?

## THE SPIRITS OF JUST MEN MADE PERFECT

Hebrews Chapter 11, which has been dubbed "the faith chapter," provides a comprehensive response to the question presented at the end of the previous section. In that regard, it offers a meaningful perspective concerning those who died before Christ's resurrection and were imputed righteousness. Certainly, when we survey the list, it includes some of the more notable men and women of the Old Testament: Abraham, Sarah, Isaac, Jacob, Moses, Rahab, David, Sampson, Samuel, and many others. However, even after providing a record of their achievements through faith, Hebrews 11:39-40 offers a remarkable conclusion, which proves that Yahweh is a God of equity:

> 39. And these all, having obtained a good report through faith, received not the promise:
>
> 40. God having provided some better thing for us, that they without us should not be made perfect.

Despite obtaining a good report through faith, those mentioned in the chapter, as well as others who were imputed righteousness, did not receive the promise. What promise did they not receive? As mentioned earlier, it was the promise of eternal redemption and eternal inheritance through Jesus Christ. On that note, to truly appreciate what the promise is, requires a comprehensive understanding of the book of Hebrews. For more on that subject, I invite you to read my book entitled *Faith: Who Hath Bewitched You?*

Overall, the book of Hebrews is explicit in its comparison between the impact of righteousness based on the law compared to the righteousness of Jesus Christ. In harmony with that conclusion, Hebrews 10:1-4 says,

1. For the law having a shadow of good things to come, and not the very image of the things, *can never with those sacrifices which they offered year by year continually make the comers thereunto perfect.*

2. For then would they not have ceased to be offered? because that the worshippers once purged should have had no more conscience of sins.

3. But in those sacrifices there is a remembrance again made of sins every year.

4. *For it is not possible that the blood of bulls and of goats should take away sins.*

First, the perfection that the law could not bring refers to being purged from sin once and for all. It speaks to an incomplete work. Under the law, redemption through the sacrifice of animals was a temporary measure performed annually, but it could not purge the conscience from dead works (Hebrews 9:9). In other words, it could not produce a change in the inner man or provide a spiritual rebirth. Hence, their spirits were not perfected. Therefore, for all those mentioned in Hebrews Chapter 11, the nature of sin still remained even though righteousness was imputed to them. Hence, Hebrews 11:40, in recognition of this, says they were not "perfected."

On the other hand, Hebrews 10:12-14 in respect to Jesus Christ's sacrifice says,

12. But this man, after he had offered one sacrifice for sins forever, sat down on the right hand of God;

13. From henceforth expecting till his enemies be made his footstool.

14. *For by one offering he hath perfected for ever them that are sanctified.*

Again, the reference to "perfected" in this passage speaks of being sanctified once and for all, which also constitutes a change in nature. It speaks of a completed work. If the blood of animals brought sanctification to the flesh, which speaks of an external work, Hebrews 9:14 by way of comparison asks a question. It says, "How much more shall the blood of Christ, who through the eternal Spirit offered himself without spot to God, purge your conscience from dead works to serve the living God?"

Unlike the sacrifices of the law, which only purified the flesh, the blood of Christ produced an internal work and cleansed our spirits. Hebrews 9:14 refers to this as Him having obtained eternal redemption for humanity. Consequently, this also results in an eternal inheritance (Hebrews 9:15). Therefore, in its entirety, "the promise" that those in Hebrews Chapter 11 did not receive was eternal redemption and eternal inheritance. This was the promise that God made to Abraham in Genesis Chapter 12. This was the "better thing" God was providing so that they without us would not be brought into a state of perfection or eternal redemption.

Based on the righteous acts performed by those mentioned in Hebrews Chapter 11, the Lord accredited them with righteousness, or better yet, He put righteousness on their account. However, this temporary measure of imputing righteousness was only implemented until Christ came. Therefore, when Christ died and fulfilled the righteous requirements of the law, those who had a credit of righteousness received the promise of eternal redemption. Hebrews 12:23 refers to this as the spirits of just men made perfect.

However, prior to this, because eternal redemption for the inner man or our spirits had not yet been accomplished, those who died with a good report or who were imputed righteousness went to paradise or Abraham's bosom until Christ came. This is why Jesus said, "Abraham rejoiced to see my day; he saw it and was glad" (John 8:56). However, as a result of Jesus' death and resurrection, which provided eternal redemption for humanity, when the righteous die, they immediately go to heaven. This is also where paradise is now located.

## God's Promise to Abraham

When God made the promise to Abraham, Genesis 15:6 says "And he believed in the Lord; and He counted it to him for righteousness." This established the premise of righteousness by faith, which is distinct from righteousness by the law. This is also the same as righteousness based on belief as opposed to righteousness established on works (Romans 10:1-11). Romans 4:13 reinforces this position by echoing the sentiments of Genesis 15:6, which says, the promise that God made to Abraham and his seed was not through the law but through the righteousness of faith. Therefore, for the promise of eternal redemption and eternal inheritance to come into play, righteousness by faith had to be enacted; this was introduced by Jesus Christ.

In reference to our previous conversation on the absence of law, Galatians 3:19 points out that the law was added because of transgression until Jesus came to fulfill the promise. Hence, before the establishment of the law, (except for murder, Genesis 9:6), there was no true indication of what constituted God's righteous requirements. In addition, the law, because of its statutes and overall ineffectiveness, determined everyone to be "under sin" (Romans 3:10), even those who were imputed righteousness.

Righteousness produced by works or by means of the law was temporal and had no impact on the inner man. In other words, as it pertained to humanity's very nature, the spirit on the inside was not altered or changed. However, Christ's sacrifice instituted the righteousness of faith, which was ascribed to Abraham. This accomplished righteousness on the inside with Hebrews 10:14 saying, "For by one offering He hath perfected forever them that are sanctified." Therefore, when Christ came and ushered in righteousness by faith, He fulfilled the promise, brought about eternal redemption and consequently, eternal inheritance (Hebrews 9:11-15).

As a summary of this discussion, when God made the promise to Abraham, he believed God, and righteousness was imputed unto him. Therefore, the fulfillment of the promise (eternal redemption and eternal inheritance) was going to be accomplished based on this premise, through the righteousness of faith. However, before the righteousness of faith came, which would fulfill the promise, righteousness was placed on the account of those who performed righteousness. Hence, once the promise was fulfilled, those who were credited with righteousness would receive the promise of eternal redemption. Subsequently, their spirits would be perfected.

## Paradise and Its Present Location

Based on the account provided by Paul in 2 Corinthians 12:1-4, paradise is located in the third heaven, where God is. However, as we have concluded, heaven was not always its location as Jesus did not go there immediately after death. The word "paradise" is the Greek *paradeisos* and it means garden. The definition also identifies it as the abode of the souls/spirits of the righteous until the resurrection of Christ. This includes the people in Hebrews Chapter 11 who were imputed righteousness before Christ's resurrection. Recall, that in Scripture, paradise is synonymous with Abraham's bosom. Therefore, the conditions that were present there resembled that of a garden. Hence, in Luke 23:43, when Jesus said to the thief on the cross, "Today, you will be with me in paradise" this is what He was referring to.

However, according to 2 Corinthians 12:4, we are presented with a different location for paradise, which is heaven. Additionally, Revelation

2:7 says. "To him that overcometh will I give to eat of the tree of life which is in the midst of the paradise of God." By mentioning the tree of life, this draws reference to the garden of Eden in Genesis 2:8. Therefore, the conditions of paradise resemble the environment that existed in the garden of Eden. Moreover, this is the same tree of life in the holy city, Jerusalem, which is presently in heaven and descends from there.

This chapter, in keeping with the title of the book, has provided a comprehensive discussion on Abraham's Bosom and the various topics related to the subject. It represents a fitting conclusion of what happens when we die from a scriptural perspective and insight into several topics that were once debatable.

# Conclusion

It was not the intent of this book to simply provide information on what happens when we die. More importantly, its purpose was to provide insight concerning death so that you can make your call and election sure (2 Peter 1:3-11). One of the greatest lies the devil has convinced the world of is that "you only live once" (YOLO). With this persuasion comes the concept of living life to its fullest because this is all there is. Paul, in his letter to the Corinthians, points out in 1 Corinthians 15:32 that if there is no resurrection of the dead or if, indeed, we only live once, then we should eat and drink, for tomorrow we die. Satan would like you to believe that there is no accountability for your actions. Nevertheless, the Word of God is quite clear that we all have to give an account of the deeds done in our bodies.

> For we must all appear before the judgment seat of Christ; that every one may receive the things done in his body, according to that he hath done, whether it be good or bad. (2 Corinthians 5:10)

I hope that reading this book has given you a better appreciation for the brevity of life, the decisions that are made, and a keener understanding of what awaits us when we cross the threshold from life into death. Additionally, this book serves as an inspiration to exercise righteous diligence in light of our eternal destiny. Indeed, it is time to awake from sleep (spiritual inactivity/slumber), for now, is our salvation nearer than when we believed.

# References

- AMG Publishers, The Hebrew-Greek Key Study Bible. Editor, Zodhiates, S. © 1995
- Strong, James © 2009 Strong's Exhaustive Concordance of the Bible.
- Who invented the comma? (2013) Retrieved from http://www.Guernseydonkey.com.
- Butler, Clement C., © 2015, The Volume of the Book: Insight into Rightly Dividing The Word.
- Strong, James © 2009 Strong's Exhaustive Concordance of the Bible.
- Strong James © 2011 Greek and Hebrew Dictionary of the Bible.
- The King James Bible
- Birth and Death Rates. Ecology Global Network Retrieved July 26, 2018 from www.ecology.com/birth-death-rates/
- Brown-Driver-Briggs, Strong's Concordance with Hebrew and Greek Lexicon
- Franklin, Benjamin., (1817) The Works of Benjamin Franklin.
- Producer, Martin Brest, Director, Martin Brest (1998) Meet Joe Black, USA, Universal Pictures.
- Producer, Douglas Wick, Producer David Franzoni, Producer Branko Lustig, Director, Ridley Scott (2000) Gladiator, USA, DreamWorks Pictures.
- Discovery World. A Wink, A Blink and A Twink. Extracted September 11, 2017 from https://www.discoveryworld.us/science/a-wink-a-blink-and-twink

- Dust [Def.] Strong's Concordance with Hebrew and Greek Lexicon Retrieved July 1, 2020 from https://www.blueletterbible.org/lang/Lexicon/Lexicon.cfm?strongs=G4832&t=KJV
- Ground [Def.] Strong's Concordance with Hebrew and Greek Lexicon Retrieved July 3, 2020 from https://www.blueletterbible.org/lang/Lexicon/Lexicon.cfm?strongs=H127&t=KJV
- Breathed [Def.] Strong's Concordance with Hebrew and Greek Lexicon Retrieved July 3, 2020 from https://www.blueletterbible.org/lang/Lexicon/Lexicon.cfm?strongs=H5301&t=KJV
- Breath [Def.] Strong's Concordance with Hebrew and Greek Lexicon Retrieved July 5, 2020 from https://www.blueletterbible.org/lang/Lexicon/Lexicon.cfm?strongs=H5397&t=KJV
- Breath [Def.] Strong's Concordance with Hebrew and Greek Lexicon Retrieved July 10, 2020 from https://www.blueletterbible.org/lang/Lexicon/Lexicon.cfm?strongs=H7307&t=KJV
- Translated [Def.] Strong's Concordance with Hebrew and Greek Lexicon Retrieved July 14, 2020 from https://www.blueletterbible.org/lang/Lexicon/Lexicon.cfm?strongs=G3346&t=KJV
- Transfigured [Def.] Strong's Concordance with Hebrew and Greek Lexicon Retrieved July 14, 2020 from https://www.blueletterbible.org/lang/Lexicon/Lexicon.cfm?strongs=G3339&t=KJV
- Quickened [Def.] Strong's Concordance with Hebrew and Greek Lexicon Retrieved July 15, 2020 from https://www.blueletterbible.org/lang/Lexicon/Lexicon.cfm?strongs=G5607&t=KJV
- Only Begotten [Def.] Strong's Concordance with Hebrew and Greek Lexicon Retrieved July 20, 2020 from https://www.blueletterbible.org/lang/Lexicon/Lexicon.cfm?strongs=G3439&t=KJV
- Mansions [Def.] Strong's Concordance with Hebrew and Greek Lexicon Retrieved July 21, 2020 from https://www.blueletterbible.org/lang/Lexicon/Lexicon.cfm?strongs=G3438&t=KJV
- Abode [Def.] Strong's Concordance with Hebrew and Greek Lexicon Retrieved July 22, 2020 from https://www.blueletterbible.org/lang/Lexicon/Lexicon.cfm?strongs=G3438&t=KJV

- House [Def.] Strong's Concordance with Hebrew and Greek Lexicon Retrieved July 23, 2020 from https://www.blueletterbible.org/lang/Lexicon/Lexicon.cfm?strongs=G3614&t=KJV
- Heaven [Def.] Strong's Concordance with Hebrew and Greek Lexicon Retrieved July 25, 2020 from https://www.blueletterbible.org/lang/Lexicon/Lexicon.cfm?strongs=H8064&t=KJV
- Hell [Def.] Strong's Concordance with Hebrew and Greek Lexicon Retrieved August 2, 2020 from h https://www.blueletterbible.org/lang/Lexicon/Lexicon.cfm?strongs=H7585&t=KJV
- Hell [Def.] Strong's Concordance with Hebrew and Greek Lexicon Retrieved August 4, 2020 from https://www.blueletterbible.org/lang/Lexicon/Lexicon.cfm?strongs=G86&t=KJV
- Hell [Def.] Strong's Concordance with Hebrew and Greek Lexicon Retrieved August 5, 2020 from https://www.blueletterbible.org/lang/Lexicon/Lexicon.cfm?strongs=G1067&t=KJV
- Hell [Def.] Strong's Concordance with Hebrew and Greek Lexicon Retrieved August 5, 2020 from https://www.blueletterbible.org/lang/Lexicon/Lexicon.cfm?strongs=G5020&t=KJV
- Bosom [Def.] Strong's Concordance with Hebrew and Greek Lexicon Retrieved August 10, 2020 from https://www.blueletterbible.org/lang/Lexicon/Lexicon.cfm?strongs=G2859&t=KJV
- Paradise [Def.] Strong's Concordance with Hebrew and Greek Lexicon Retrieved August 17, 2020 from https://www.blueletterbible.org/lang/Lexicon/Lexicon.cfm?strongs=G3857&t=KJV
- Booth, Dawn, photographer, "Armor of God" [Contenders for the Faith]. Photograph. 2010. Retrieved December 9, 2020 from https://www.google.com/search?rlz=1C-1CHBF_enBS731BS752&source=univ&tbm=isch&q=dawn+booth+photo+of+the+whole+armor+of+God&sa=X&ved=2ahUKEwi7yvq-gsTtAhXkAp0JHVPXCNUQjJkEegQIBRAB&biw=1536&bih=755#imgrc=jul37HAxzbtFjM.

# About the Author

Clement C. Butler is an author and teacher who resides in Nassau, Bahamas. He is a graduate of The Principles of Life Bible College and has a bachelor's degree in Biblical Hermeneutics and Leadership. In 2016, he founded Approved Workman Ministries which is based on the principle of 2 Timothy 2:15. It is a teaching ministry dedicated to bringing the enlightenment of Scripture and knowledge of the kingdom of God. To accomplish this, he has written a collection of books that he calls "The Teacher's Series."

Please check out other books of "The Teacher's Series"

The Volume of the Book: Insights into Rightly Dividing the Word of Truth.

God's Eternal Purpose Volume One: The Establishment of God's Kingdom.

God's Eternal Purpose Volume Two: The identity of the sons of God: The Image of Jesus Christ.

Freedom: The True Perspective About Women in Ministry.

Are There *Really* Mansions in Heaven? It's a Family Affair

The Five-fold Ministry Gifts: Understanding the Gifts of Christ in Light of God's Purpose

Please visit our website: www.approvedworkmanministries.com
Please visit our website:
www.approvedworkmanmininstires.com

Follow us on Twitter: @242teacher

www.ingramcontent.com/pod-product-compliance
Lightning Source LLC
Chambersburg PA
CBHW070456090426
42735CB00012B/2575